929
51263

NAMES

AND THEIR MEANING

NAMES

AND THEIR MEANING

LEOPOLD WAGNER

TYNRON PRESS
SCOTLAND

© *This edition, Tynron Press, 1989*

First published in this edition in 1989 by
Tynron Press
Stenhouse
Thornhill
Dumfriesshire DG3 4LD
Scotland

ISBN 1-871948-51-7

Cover design by John Hall
Printed in Singapore by Fong & Sons Printers Pte. Ltd.

INTRODUCTION.

NOT the least difficult matter in connection with the present work has been the choice of a title. The one finally determined upon is far from satisfactory, because it scarcely suggests the scope of the subject treated. True enough, the single word NOMENCLATURE offered itself as a suitable title; but this is really a French word, derived, of course, from the Latin, and although it has been admitted into our vocabulary simply owing to the lack of an English equivalent, its use is properly restricted to the classification of technical terms in relation to a particular branch of science. In a scientific sense, then, the word Nomenclature finds a ready acceptance; but for the classification of the names of persons, of places, and of things, it is altogether too pedantic. A young friend of the author the other day, on being informed, in answer to his inquiry, that this work would probably be entitled " The Curiosities of Nomenclature," promptly asked whether it might not be as well to explain, first of all, what the word Nomenclature meant. Now, the author does not believe for one moment that any intelligent person

who took up this volume would be at a loss to judge
of its contents from the title, that is, supposing the
word Nomenclature appeared on the page ; nevertheless, his young friend's suggestion reminded him
that a book intended not for the scientific and
learned, but for general reference, should bear a
title easily comprehended by all classes of the community. The title originally chosen has, therefore,
been rejected in favour of one less pretentious and
more matter-of-fact : if it is not sufficiently expressive, the fault must be attributed to the poverty of
the English language.

Of all the " Ologies," PHILOLOGY, or the science of
language, is the most seductive ; and that branch of
it known as ETYMOLOGY, which traces the derivation
and combination of the words of a language from
its primary roots, possesses an interest—one might
almost say a fascination—for all, when once the
attention has been arrested by it. This fact is
proved by the popularity of Archbishop Trench's
published lectures on " The Study of Words," which
have now reached a nineteenth edition. But it is
not to an examination of the dictionary words of the
English language that the present volume is devoted.
Bearing in mind that several excellent works already
exist on this subject, the author has occupied
himself in the following pages exclusively with the
etymology, and significance of NAMES—of *personal
names*, comprising Surnames, Sobriquets, Pseu-
donyms, Nicknames, Class Names, and Professional
Designations ; of *names of places*, including the

Countries of the World, with the principal
Seas, Islands, Gulfs, Straits, &c., the United
States of North America, the Counties of England
and Wales, and particularly the Districts, Streets,
Squares, Churches, and Public Buildings of London ;
of the names of Religious Sects and Political Factions ; of the names of Inns and Taverns ; in addition
to the names of an infinite number of objects with
which every one is familiar, but whose actual significance is comprehended only by a few.

As to the utility of such a work, a brief glance into
these pages may convince the reader that the subject
of NAMES is fraught with much popular interest.
Take the names of London streets. How many
among the thousands who follow their daily occupations within sight of the gilt cross of St. Paul's,
ever reflect that the name of each street they frequent and pass by the way, points to the origin of
the street itself: and that, were they to cultivate a
practical acquaintance with those names, their knowledge of English History and Sociology might be
considerably enlarged, with a result that they would
be brought to ask themselves at length how they
could have been possessed of " souls so dead " as
never to have entered upon such a profitable field
of inquiry before ? Whitefriars, Blackfriars, and
Austin Friars, carry us back in imagination to the
days of yore ; the friars have long returned to the
dust, but the localities they inhabited are still identified with their existence by the names they bear.
Yet these are possibly the only thoroughfares in the

City—with the exception of such as have derived their names from a neighbouring church, public building, or private mansion—concerning which the average Londoner can express himself with any degree of certainty: if he venture a guess at the rest, it is safe to assert that he will be open to correction. The like observation applies to public buildings.

If the question were asked, for example, why the well-known Ships' Registry Offices over the Royal Exchange are universally referred to as "Lloyd's," ninety-nine out of every hundred City men would avail themselves of the very plausible suggestion that the system of Marine Insurance was first established, either there or elsewhere, by some person named Lloyd. True, a certain Edward Lloyd had a remote connection with the enterprise; but he was a coffee-house keeper, who probably knew no more about ships and their tonnage than "Jonathan," another noted London coffee-house keeper, after whom the Stock Exchange was formerly designated, knew about "bulls" and "bears." Again, it is not every one who could account, off hand, for such familiar names as Scotland Yard, Bedlam, Doctors' Commons, the Charterhouse, the churches of St. Mary-Axe, St. Clement-Danes, St. Hallow's-Barking, or St. Catherine Cree. A few barristers would, doubtless, be in a position to inform us wherefore our seminaries for the study of the law were originally styled "Inns of Court"; but the ordinary inquirer, left to his own resources, might

find the problem somewhat difficult to solve. Surely
they were not at one time inns? and if so, whence
came the designation Inns of Court? Did the Court
flunkeys patronize them, perhaps? Or, more likely,
did the sovereign, attended by the Court, take a fancy
to sleeping beneath the roof of each for once in a way,
after the manner of Queen Elizabeth? And, speaking about inns, every Londoner is, of course, aware
of the one-time existence of "La Belle Sauvage" on
the north side of Ludgate Hill, albeit the origin of
this sign has generally been ascribed to Pocahontas,
of Virginia, who accompanied her husband, John
Rolfe, back to England in the year 1616, and, as
tradition has it, put up at this famous old coaching-
house. Moreover, Messrs. Cassell and Co., whose premises occupy the site, and are approached from La
Belle Sauvage Yard, have profited by the popular
misconception to the extent of adopting the figure of
a female partly clad in skins as their trade-mark.
Then, again, who has not heard of "The Tabard"?
and whence did that derive its sign? Among other
celebrated inns still preserved to us, we have
"Jack Straw's Castle" on Hampstead Heath. But
who was Jack Straw? and had he ever a castle
thereabouts? As will be shown in these pages, the
answer to these questions is associated with a very
stirring moment in English History.

A great deal of the early history of England can
be gleaned from the names of the counties into
which this country is divided. The terms Shire
and County are so far synonymous in that they

indicate a portion of land distinguished by a particular name; yet, etymologically considered, they
are widely different. Although every shire is a
county, it is not every county to whose individual
name the word "shire" may be added. The latter is
essentially Anglo-Saxon, denoting a division of land
possessed by an earl, and wherever it occurs it points
conclusively to the Saxon occupation of England.
Certainly, we do not speak of Essex-shire, Middle-
sex-shire, or Sussex-shire, because the Saxon territories referred to, as well as their relative positions,
are fully indicated in the names themselves. Neither
are we accustomed to allude to Surrey-shire, for the
reason that the word *Surrey* expressed the Anglo-
Saxon for the land south of the *rey*, or river,
comprising, as it did, that large tract of land described as Wessex, or the land of the West Saxons,
now divided into six southern shires. The fact is,
Wessex was the great kingdom of the Saxons in this
country, whereas Essex, Middlesex, and Sussex were
but petty kingdoms. Consequently, in the kingdom
of Wessex it was that earldoms were first created,
and lands appertaining thereto were literally *scired*,
or sheared off. On the other hand, it would be
ridiculous in the extreme, quite apart from the
unfamiliarity of such an expression, to speak of
Kent-shire, because there is nothing in the name
that invests it with a Saxon interest. The same remark is applicable to Cornwall. It is only from habit,
too, or because the name lends itself to the euphony,
that Devon is denominated a shire; for not only

is this a Celtic name, but the Saxons scarcely penetrated into, and certainly never occupied any considerable portion of, the county. The England of the Saxons, therefore, is to be distinguished wherever the word "shire" appears as part of the name of a county.

If the foregoing paragraph be deemed interesting to the general inquirer, a careful digest of the chapter on "The Countries of the World" should prove most instructive. With a few exceptions only, the names of the different countries of the Old World afford us an indication of their original inhabitants, or the rude tribes that overran them. In regard to the New World, such names of countries as are not of native origin invariably point to the nationality of the navigators who discovered them or of the adventurers who explored and colonized them. The maritime enterprise of the Spanish and Portuguese is in nothing so evident as in the territories named in accordance with their respective languages in South and Central America, to say nothing of the islands discovered by them in the Atlantic and Pacific Oceans. And, as a set-off against the shameful treatment by the Spaniards of Christopher Columbus, it must not be forgotten that the whole of the North American territory now embraced in the United States was originally designated Columbia in his honour, which name has been preserved in the Western portion of the continent known as British Columbia. A few Spanish names still linger in North America, notably California, Labrador,

Florida, Nevada, Oregon, and Colorado. But the Spaniards were rovers rather than settlers; wherefore they contented themselves with maintaining their national reputation as successful navigators by giving names to the countries they discovered, and establishing a lucrative trading monopoly in that portion of the Caribbean Sea which formerly bore the name of the Spanish Main.

On the contrary, the English and French have distinguished themselves always, and all the world over, as colonists ; so that, saving those States of North America which have received the native names of the great lakes and rivers, we can discover exactly which were colonized by the one nation and which by the other. Moreover, the English and French have generally exercised the common trait of honouring the mother country by naming a new colony or a newly-discovered island after the reigning monarch or a distinguished countryman. A similar trait in the Dutch character presents itself in the repetition of the names of the native places of their navigators and colonists; while the Spaniards and Portuguese have displayed a tendency for naming an island discovered or a river explored by them in a manner commemorative of the day that witnessed the event. At the same time, it would not be wise to conjecture, merely from the name, that Columbus discovered the island of Trinidad on the Feast of the Holy Trinity, because he did nothing of the kind. Therefore, it behoves the curious inquirer to make himself acquainted with the circumstances under which our geographical names have arisen, so as to avoid falling into error. As well might he maintain, without the requisite knowledge, that the Canary Islands owed their designation to the birds that have so long been exported thence; for although such a conclusion were extremely plausible, he would still be at a loss to know how the canaries came by their name in the first place.

A like difficulty is liable to be encountered relative to the Sandwich Islands. A particularly smart boy might, indeed, be expected to inform us, as the outcome of a hastily-formed opinion, that the Sandwich Islands were so called because a shipwrecked crew who once found a refuge thereon continued to support themselves until such time as they were rescued by a passing vessel upon sandwiches. The bare idea may be laughed at; but it is no more preposterous than that the Canary Islands received their name from the birds that are found there in such plenty. The question at issue furnishes an example as to how a name may be perpetuated in different ways. Thus, Captain Cook named the Sandwich Islands in compliment to John Montague, fourth Earl of Sandwich and First Lord of the Admiralty, who took his title from Sandwich, or, as the etymology of this place implies, the "sand town," one of the ancient Cinque Ports in Kent. An inveterate gamester was this Lord Sandwich; so much so that he would sit at the gaming-table for thirty hours and more at a stretch, never desisting from the game to partake of a meal, but from time to time ordering the waiter to bring him some slices of meat placed between two slices of thin bread, from which circumstance this convenient form of refreshment received the name of Sandwiches.

Mention of sandwiches reminds us that very few tradesmen possess the remotest idea of the significance of the names of the various commodities in which they deal. Ask a purveyor of ham and beef to explain the origin of the word Sandwich, and he will be quite unable to furnish an answer. Put a similar question to a Tobacconist, and it will be found that he has never interested himself to the extent of inquiring what the word Tobacco means, not to speak of the names of the different kinds of tobacco. A Haberdasher, again, would be sorely perplexed to account for his individual trade-name; so would a Milliner, so would a Grocer, so would a Tailor; and so would almost every one who passes for an intelligent citizen, yet whose reflections have never been directed toward those trifling concerns which, as one might be led to suppose, are most immediately interesting to him. And so we might go on multiplying examples until this Introduction reached an altogether inordinate length, with no other object than to arouse the reader's interest in the pages that follow. But the necessity for a more extended Introduction does not arise. The scope of this work will be sufficiently indicated by the Analytical Table of Contents; but even there a very large number of names incidentally referred to in the text have not been included. The Index may be somewhat more to the purpose, inasmuch as every item set forth therein will be found not merely alluded to but discussed in the book; and to the book itself the reader is now referred.

L. W.

LONDON.

CONTENTS.

———◆◆———

18 Contents.

Contents. 19

ROYAL SURNAMES.

NATIONAL NICKNAMES.

BIRDS.

RELIGIOUS ORDERS.

PAPER AND PRINTING.

POLITICAL NICKNAMES.

Contents.

FLOWERS.

THE BIBLE.

WINES.

LITERARY SOBRIQUETS.

Contents.

LONDON DISTRICTS AND SUBURBS.

BATTLES.

NOTABLE DAYS AND FESTIVALS.

TEXTILES, EMBROIDERIES, AND LACE.

CLASS NAMES AND NICKNAMES.

Spinster, Widow, Grass Widow, Chaperon, Duenna, Dowager; Blue Stocking, Abigail, Grisette, Colleen; Milliner, Haberdasher, Grocer, Greengrocer, Boniface, Ostler; Cordwainer, Tailor, Tallyman, Uncle, Barber, Barber-Surgeon; Arcadian, Mentor, Usher, Bachelor; Beefeaters, Police, Bobbies, Peelers, Bow Street

THE COUNTRIES OF THE WORLD.

THE oldest of the four great divisions of the world received its modern designation **Asia** from the Sanskrit *Ushas*, signifying "land of the dawn." **Africa** traces its origin to the Phœnician *afer*, a black man, and the Sanskrit *ac*, the earth, a country. **Europe** owes its name to the Greek *eurus*, broad, and *op*, to see, or *ops*, the face, in allusion to " the broad face of the earth." **America** honours the memory of Amerigo Vespucci, the Florentine navigator, who landed on the New Continent south of the Equator, the year after Columbus discovered the northern mainland in 1498. The name of America first appeared in a work published by Waldsemüller at St. Die, in Lorraine, in the year 1507. It is worthy of note that when Columbus landed in America he imagined he had set foot on part of that vast territory east of the Ganges vaguely known as India; therefore he gave the name of **Indians** to the aborigines. This also accounts for the islands in the Caribbean Sea being styled the **West Indies**.

The cradle of the human race bears the name of **Palestine,** or in Hebrew *Palestina*, meaning "the land of strangers," agreeably to the native word

palash, to wander.   Palestine is usually denominated
the **Holy Land,** because it was the scene of the
birth, life, and death of the Redeemer. **Asia
Minor** is, of course, Lesser Asia.

For the title of **Persia** we are indebted to the
Greeks, who gave the name of *Persis* to the region
(of which the capital was *Persipolis*) originally over-
run by a wild branch of the Ayrian race called the
Parsa, meaning, in the native tongue, " the Tigers "
[*see* PARSEES].   The suffix *ia,* wherever it occurs in
a geographical sense, expresses the Celtic for land
or territory.   Hence, Persia signifies the territory of
the Parsa or Parsees ; **Arabia,** the country of the
Arabs, " men of the desert " ; **Abyssinia,** that of the
Abassins, or " mixed races " ; **Kaffraria,** that of the
Kaffirs, or " unbelievers" ; and **Ethiopia,** the "land
of the blacks," according to the two Greek words
aithein, to burn, and *ops,* the face.   **India** denotes
the country traversed by the **Indus,** or rather the
Hindu, which name is a Persicized form of the
Sanskrit *Sindhu,* " a great river," rendered *Hindus* in
the Greek.   Synonymous with the Celtic suffix just
discussed is the Persian *stan :* consequently **Hindu-
stan** signifies the territory traversed by the river
Hindu, and peopled by the Hindoos ; **Turkestan,**
the country of the Turks ; **Afghanistan,** that of
the Afghans ; **Beloochistan,** that of the Belooches ;
and **Kurdestan,** properly **Koordistan,** that of the
Koords.   The term **China** is a western corruption
of Tsina, so called in honour of Tsin, the founder
of the great dynasty which commenced in the third

century B.C., when a knowledge of this country was
first conveyed to the Western nations. It was this
Tsin who built the Great Wall of China (or Tsin) to
keep out the Barbarians. The Chinese Empire bears
the description of the **Celestial Empire** because its
early rulers were all celestial deities. **Siberia** is a
term indicative of *Siber*, the residence of Kutsheen
Khan, the celebrated Tartar prince, recognized as
the ancient capital of the Tartars, the ruins of
which may still be seen. Here again the Celtic
suffix *ia* has reference to the surrounding territory.

Russia constituted the country of the Russ, a
tribe who overran it at a very early period. The
Russian Empire was founded by Ruric, or Rourik, a
Scandinavian chief whose death took place in the
year A.D., 879. **Circassia** denotes the country of the
Tcherkes, a Tartar tribe who settled in the neighbourhood of the river Terck. The **Crimea** received
its name from a small town established in the peninsula by the Kimri, or Cymri, and known to the Greeks
as *Kimmerikon*. **Finland** is properly Fenland, "the
land of marshes." **Sweden** is a modern term made
up of the Latin *Suedia*, signifying the land of the
Suevi, a warlike tribe of the Goths, and the Anglo-
Saxon *den*, testifying to its occupation by the Danes.
Norway shows the result of a gradual modification
of the Anglo-Saxon *Norea*, and the original *Nordoe*,
being the Scandinavian for "north island." It is
easy to understand in this connection how the old
Norsemen, deterred by the intense cold of the Arctic
Sea, took it for granted that the great northern

peninsula was surrounded by water, without actually determining the fact. The native name of this country in modern times is *Nordrike, i.e.,* the north kingdom.

Britain was known to the Phœnicians as *Barat-Anac,* or " the land of tin," as far back as the year 1037 B.C. Some five hundred years afterwards the Island was alluded to by the Romans under the name of Britannia, which subsequently became shortened into Britain. **England** was originally *Engaland,* the land of the Engles, or Angles, who came over from Sleswick, a province of Jutland. Prior to the year 258, which witnessed its invasion by the Scoti, a tribe who inhabited the northern portions of the country now known as Ireland, **Scotland** bore the name of **Caledonia,** literally the hilly country of the Caels, or Gaels. The word Cael, or Gael, is a corruption of *Gadhel,* signifying in the native tongue " a hidden rover " ; while Scot, derived from the native *scuite,* means practically the same thing, *i.e.,* a wanderer. The Caledonians were the inhabitants of the Highlands, the termination *dun* expressing the Celtic for a hill, fort, stronghold ; the Scots were the invaders from **Scotia**, who appropriated the Hebrides and the Western Islands ; whereas the Lowlanders were the Picts, so called from their description by the Romans, *picti,* painted men. These Picts were eventually subdued by the Caledonians and Britons from their respective sides. The Gaelic designation of what is now **Ireland** was *Ierne,* indicative of the " western isle." Ireland is commonly styled **The Emerald Isle** owing to its fresh verdure.

Wales was originally **Cambria**, so called on account of the Cymri, or Kimri, who peopled it. The modern title of **Wales** was given to this province by the Anglo-Saxons, because they regarded it, in common with Cornwall, as the land of foreigners. Traces of the Wahl or Welsh still present themselves in such names as Wallachia, Walcheren, Walloon, Wallingford, Welshpool, &c. Thus we see that the prenomen *Wahl*, subject to slight modifications in the spelling, denotes any foreign settlement from the Saxon point of view. The Saxons, by the way, whose original settlement is determined by the little kingdom of **Saxony,** derived their name from the *seax,* or short crooked knife with which they armed themselves.

France was known to the Greeks as *Gallatia*, and to the Romans as *Gallia*, afterwards modified into **Gaul,** because it was the territory of the Celtiæ, or Celts. The modern settlers of the country were the Franks, so called from the *franca*, a kind of javelin which they carried, who in the fifth century inhabited the German province of **Franconia,** and, travelling westwards, gradually accomplished the conquest of Gaul. **France,** therefore, signifies the country of the Franks, or, as the Germans call it, *Frankreich*, *i.e.*, the Kingdom of the Franks. All the western nations were styled Franks by the Turks and Orientals, and anything brought to them from the west invariably merited a prenomen descriptive of its origin, as, for example, FRANKINCENSE, by which was meant incense brought from the country of the Franks. **Normandy** indicates the coast settlement of the Northmen, or Danes; while **Brittany** comprised the land appropriated by the kings of Britain.

Germany was in ancient times known as Tronges, or the country of the Tungri, a Latin word signifying "speakers"; but the Romans afterwards gave it the name of Germanus, which was a Latinized Celtic term meaning "neighbours," originally bestowed by the Gauls upon the warlike people beyond the Rhine. **Holland** is the modern acceptation of *Ollant*, the Danish for "marshy ground"; whereas **Belgium** denotes the land of the Belgiæ. The fact that the term **Netherlands** is expressive of the low countries need scarcely detain us. **Denmark** is properly Danmark, *i.e.*, the territory comprised within the *marc*, or boundary established by Dan, the Scandinavian chieftain. **Jutland** means the land of the Jutes, a family of the Goths who settled in this portion of Denmark. **Prussia** is a corruption of *Borussia*, the country of the Borussi; and **Bohemia,** the country of the Boii, just as **Hungary** was originally inhabited by the Huns, a warlike Asiatic family, who expelled the Goths from this territory in the year 376. These Huns were first heard of in China in the third century B.C. under the name of *Hiong-nu*, meaning "giants." **Poland** is an inversion of *Land-Pole*, the Slavonic for "men of the plains," who first overran this territory.

Servia was styled by the Romans *Suedia,* the district peopled by the Suevi before they were driven northwards to their final settlement in the territory now called Sweden. **Montenegro** literally indicates "black mountain." **Bosnia** is the country traversed by the river Bosna; **Moldavia,** that traversed by the Moldau; and **Moravia,** that traversed by the Morava. **Bulgaria** is a modern corruption of *Volgaria,* meaning the country peopled by the Volsci; while **Roumania** was anciently a Roman province. **Turkey** is more correctly written *Turkia,* the country of the Turks. This country also bears the style of the **Ottoman Empire,** in honour of Othman I., who assumed the government of the empire about the year 1300. **Greece** is the modern form of the Latin *Grœcia,* from the Greek *Graikoi,* a name originally bestowed upon the inhabitants of Hellas.

Austria is our mode of describing the *Oesterreich,* literally the Eastern Empire, in contradistinction to the Western Empire founded by Charlemagne. **Italy** was so called after Italus, one of the early kings of that country. **Switzerland** is an Anglicized form of the native Schweitz, the name of the three forest cantons whose people asserted their independence of Austria, afterwards applied to the whole country. **Spain** expresses the English of *Hispania,* a designation founded upon the Punic *span,* a rabbit, owing to the number of wild rabbits found in this peninsula by the Carthaginians. The ancient name of the country was *Iberia,* so styled from the Iberi, a tribe who settled in the vicinity of the river Ebro

Portugal was the *Portus Cale,* literally " the port Cale " of the Romans, the ancient name of the city of Oporto.

Algiers is a modified spelling of the Arabic *Al Jezair,* meaning " the peninsula." **Tunis** was anciently known as Tunentum, the land of the Tunes ; **Morocco** signifies the territory of the Moors; and **Barbary**; that of the Berbers. The term **Sahara** is Arabic for " desert"; while the **Soudan** denotes, according to the Arabic *Belad-ez-Suden,* the " district of the blacks." **Egypt** expresses the Hebrew for " the land of oppression," alluding to the bondage of the Israelites. **Senegambia** was originally so named owing to its situation between the Senegal and Gambia rivers. The **Gold Coast** is that portion of Guinea on the West Coast of Africa where gold is found. **Guinea** is a native West African term meaning " abounding in gold." In **Zanzibar,** properly written *Zanguebar,* we have an inversion of the Arabic *Ber-ez-Zing,* the " coast of the negroes." **Zululand** is the country of the Zulus. By the **Transvaal** is meant the territory beyond the river Vaal ; just as in Europe the Hungarians call a portion of their country TRANSYLVANIA, from its situation " beyond the wood." **Natal** received its name from Vasco di Gama because he discovered it on the Feast of the Nativity. The settlements of the Dutch Boers in South Africa are designated the **Orange Free States** from the circumstance that their original settlers were emigrants from the Principality of

Orange, in Holland. **Cape Colony** is the British colony in South Africa, so called after the Dutch settlement at Cape Town, which dates from the year 1652. The **Cape of Good Hope,** discovered by Bartholomew de Diaz in 1487, was so named (*Cabo de Bon Espérance*) by John II., King of Portugal, who, finding that Diaz had reached the extremity of Africa, regarded it as a favourable augury for future maritime enterprises.

The most southern point of South America was called Cape Hoorn (or, according to the English, **Cape Horn**) by Schonten, who first rounded it in 1616, after Hoorn, his native place in North Holland. **Patagonia** was so styled by Mageiian in accordance with the Spanish word *patagon,* meaning a large, clumsy foot. It was from the fact of seeing the impressions of the large shoes (not, as he imagined, the feet) of the aborigines that he at once concluded the country must be inhabited by giants. **Chili** is a Peruvian word denoting the "land of snow." **Argentina,** now the **Argentine Republic,** owes its name to the silvery reflection of its rivers. **Brazil** is a Portuguese term derived from *braza,* " a live coal," relative to the red dye-wood with which the country abounds. **Bolivia** perpetuates the memory of General Simon Bolivar, "the Liberator of Peru." **Uraguay** and **Paraguay** are both names of rivers ; the former meaning "the golden water," and the latter " the river of waters," referring to its numerous tributaries. **Peru** likewise received its name from its principal river, the Rio Paro, upon which stands the ancient city of Paruru. The Brazilian term *Para*, however modified, is at all times suggestive of a river. **Pernambuco** means " the mouth of hell," in allusion to the violent surf always distinguished at the mouth of its chief river. **Ecuador** is Spanish for Equator, so called by virtue of its geographical position. **Columbia** was named in honour of Christopher Columbus. **Venezuela** expresses the Spanish for " Little Venice," which designation was given to this country owing to the discovery of some Indian villages built upon piles after the manner of the " Silent City " on the Adriatic Sea.

The term **Panama** is Caribbean, indicative of the mud fish that abound in the waters on both sides of the isthmus. **Costa Rica** is literal Spanish for " rich coast " ; while **Honduras** signifies, in the same tongue, " deep water." The name of **Nicaragua** was first given by Gil Gonzales de Arila in 1521 to the great lake situated in the region now called after it, in consequence of his friendly reception by the *Cacique*, a Haytian term for a chief, whose own name was Nicaro, of a tribe of West Indians, with whom he fell in on the borders of the lake referred to. The **Mosquito Coast** owes its name to the troublesome insects (Spanish *mosca*, from the Latin *musca*, a fly) which infest this neighbourhood. **Yutacan** is a compound Indian word meaning " What do you say ? " which was the only answer the Spaniards could obtain from the natives to their inquiries concerning a description of the country.

Quatemala is a European rendering of the Mexican *quahtemali*, signifying "a decayed log of wood"; so called by the Mexican Indians who accompanied Alvarado into this region, because they found an old worm-eaten tree near the ancient palace of the Kings, or *Kachiquel*, which was thought to be the centre of the country.

Mexico denotes the place or seat of Mexitli, the Aztec God of War. The name of **California,** derived from the two Spanish words, *Caliente For-nalla, i.e.,* "hot furnace," was given by Cortez in the year 1535 to the peninsula now known as Old or Lower California, of which he was the discoverer, on account of its hot climate. **British Columbia** is the only portion of North America that retains the name of the discoverer of the New World; but originally the whole of the territory now comprised in the United States bore the designation of **Co-lumbia** in honour of Christopher Columbus. The term **Canada** is Indian, indicative of a "collection of huts"; **Manitoba** traces its origin from Manitou, the Indian appellation of "The Great Spirit." **Ontario** comes from the native *Onontac,* "the village on the mountain," and chief seat of the Onondagas; while **Quebec** is an Algonquin term signifying "take care of the rock." **Labrador** was originally denominated *Tierra Labrador*, the Spanish for "cultivated land," as distinguished from the non-fertile though moss-covered **Greenland. New Brunswick,** colonized in 1785, received its name in compliment to the House of Brunswick. **Nova**

Scotia, otherwise New Scotland, was so called by Sir William Alexander, a Scotsman who obtained a grant of this colony from James I. in 1621. **Florida** was named by Ponce de Leon in accordance with the day of its discovery, to wit, Easter Sunday, which in the Spanish language is styled *Pascua Florida.*

The first British settlement in North America was claimed by Sir Walter Raleigh on the 13th of July, 1584, in the name of Queen Elizabeth, and called **Virginia** in her honour. **Maryland** was so denominated by Lord Baltimore (who gave the name of **Baltimore** to a neighbouring State), in honour of Henrietta Maria, Queen of Charles I. **Pennsylvania** denotes the colony founded "in the wood" by William Penn, the son of Admiral Penn, in 1681. This is usually alluded to as the KEYSTONE STATE, from its relative position to the other States. **Georgia** was named after George II., in whose reign this state was colonized; and **Carolina** (North and South) after Carolus II., the Latanized style of Charles II., by whom this state was granted to eight of his favourites. **Louisiana** was so called by M. de la Sale in the year 1682, in honour of Louis XIV. of France; while **Maine** and **New Orleans** received the names of existing French provinces. The title of **New Hampshire** was given to the state granted to him in 1629 by John Mason, in compliment to his native county in England; **New Jersey** complimented the scene of action whereon Sir George Carterat distinguished himself in the defence of

Jersey Island against the Parliamentary forces in 1664; and **New York** (State) was denominated in honour of James, Duke of York, afterwards James II. [For **Michigan** see the great lake of the same name.] **Indiana** derived its name from the great number of Indians found here. **Alabama** in the native tongue, signifies " Here we rest "; **Nebraska** means " water valley"; **Ohio** is " beautiful "; **Massachusetts,** "about the great hills "; **Wisconsin,** " wild rushing channel"; **Kansas,** " smoky water "; **Tennessee,** " river of the great bend "; **Kentucky,** " at the head of a river "; **Mississippi,** " great and long river "; **Missouri,** " muddy river "; and **Minnesota,** "white water." **Arkansas** conveys the same meaning as Kansas, with the addition of the French prefix *arc,* a bow. **Illinois** is a compound of the Indian *illum,* men, and the French suffix *oix,* a tribe. **Oregon** received its name from the Spanish *oregano,* wild majoram, which grows in abundance on this portion of the Pacific shore. **Texas** means " the place of protection," in reference to the fact that a colony of French refugees were afforded protection here by General Lallemont in 1817; **Vermont** is, more correctly, *Verd Mont,* so called in testimony to the verdure-clad mountains which traverse this state; **Colorado** expresses the Spanish for " coloured, " alluding to its coloured ranges; while **Nevada** is Spanish for " snowy," indicative of the character of its mountain ridges, the *Sierra Nevada.* **Connecticut** presents itself in the native Indian form *Quinnitukut,* meaning " the country of the long river"; **Iowa** is a French corruption of a Sioux term, signifying "drowsy," or "the sleepy ones," applied to the Pahoja, or Gray-snow tribe; **Astoria** was founded by John Jacob Astor, of New York, as a fur-trading station in the year 1811; and **Delaware** received its name from Thomas West, Lord de La Warre, Governor of Virginia, who visited the bay in 1610, and died on board his vessel at its mouth.

Lake Superior denotes the uppermost and chief of the five great lakes of North America. **Lake Erie** is the Lake of the "Wild Cat," the name given to a fierce tribe of Indians exterminated by the Iroquois. **Lake Huron** owes its name to the French word *hure*, a head of hair; in reference to the Wyandots, whom the French settlers designated Hurons owing to their profusion of hair. **Lake Ontario** bears the denomination of the Canadian territory already discussed. **Niagara,** or rather, to give it its full name, *Oni-aw-garah,* expresses the West Indian for "the thunder of waters." **Lake Michigan** signifies in the native tongue "a weir for fish"; and **Lake Winnipeg,** "lake of the turbid water." The **Great Bear Lake** is indebted for its name to its northern situation [*see* ARCTIC OCEAN]; and the **Great Salt Lake,** to the saline character of its waters.

Having disposed of the different countries, let us now consider the nomenclature of the principal seas and islands.

The **Arctic Ocean** received its name pursuant to

the Greek *arktos,* a bear, on account of the northern constellations of the Great and Little Bear. The **Antarctic Ocean** denotes the ocean *anti,* against, or opposite to, the Arctic Ocean. The **Atlantic Ocean,** known to the Greeks by the name of *Atlantikos pelagos,* was originally so called from the Isle of Atlantes, which both Plato and Homer imagined to be situated beyond the Straits of Gibraltar. The **Pacific Ocean** was so named by Magellan, owing to its calm and pacific character, in striking contrast to his tempestuous passage through the Straits of Magellan, from which he emerged November 27, 1520. The **Caribbean Sea** washes the territory of the Caribbs, whose name means " cruel men." The **Mediterranean Sea** expresses the Latin (*medius,* middle, and *terra,* earth) for the sea between two continents, viz., Europe and Africa. The **Adriatic Sea** indicates the Sea of Adrian or Hadrian. The **Baltic Sea** denotes, in accordance with the Swedish *bält,* a strait, a sea full of belts, or straits. The **North Sea,** the **German Ocean,** the **Indian Ocean,** and the **Irish Sea,** are names indicative of the positions of these respective seas. The **White Sea** is so called from its proximity to sterile regions of snow and ice ; the **Black Sea,** because it abounds with black rocks ; the **Red Sea,** on account of the red soil which forms its bottom ; the **Green Sea,** owing to a strip of green always discernible along the Arabian shore ; the **Yellow Sea,** from the immense quantity of alluvial soil continually poured into it by the Yang-tse-Kiang river ; and the **Dead Sea,** because no fish of any kind has ever been found in its waters. The **Caspian Sea** preserves the name of the Caspii, a tribe who originally formed a settlement on its shores. The **Sea of Marmora** owes its designation to a small island at its western extremity which has long been famous for its marble (Latin *marmor*) quarries. The **Gulf Stream** is a warm current of water that issues from the mouth of the Amazon, immediately under the Equator, and after traversing the coast of South America, the Caribbean Sea, the Gulf of Mexico, and the coast of the United States, makes its way across the Atlantic directly for the British Isles, raising the temperature of the water through which it passes. The **Horse Latitudes,** situated between the trade winds and the westerly winds of higher latitudes, and distinguished for tedious calms, received this name because it was in this portion of the Atlantic the old navigators often threw overboard the horses which they had undertaken to transport to the West Indies. The southern banks of the West India Islands, and the water extending for some distance into the Caribbean Sea, were formerly known as the **Spanish Main,** from the fact that the Spaniards confined their buccaneering enterprises to this locality.

Hudson's Bay and **Hudson's Strait** were named after their re-discovery by Captain Henry Hudson while searching for the north-west passage in 1610. Prior to this date the Bay and the Strait had not been navigated since their original discovery by Cabot in 1512. **James' Bay** honours the memory of James

I., in whose reign it was completely explored. Quite a number of straits, gulfs, and bays bear the names of their respective navigators; therefore these need not detain us here. An exception exists in the case of **Barrow's Strait,** which was so called by Captain Penny in compliment to John Barrow, the son of Sir John Barrow the traveller and statesman, in 1850. **All Saints' Bay** was discovered by Vespucci on the Feast of All Saints in the year 1503. The **Gulf of St. Lawrence** was first explored, and the navigation of the long river of the same name commenced, on the Feast of St. Lawrence, 1500. The **Gulf of Carpentaria** preserves the memory of a Dutch captain named Carpenter who discovered it in 1606. **Torres Strait** received the name of the Spanish navigator, L. V. de Torres, to whom its discovery was due, in the year 1606. **Botany Bay** was so called by Captain Cook from the great variety of plants which he found growing on its shores when exploring it in the year 1770. The **St. George's Channel** was named after the patron saint of England. The **Skagerrack** denotes the "crooked strait between the Skagen" (so called from the Gothic *skaga,* a promontory), which forms the northern extremity of Jutland and Norway. **Zuyder Zee** expresses the Dutch for the "south sea," in relation to the North Sea or German Ocean. The **Bay of Biscay** takes its name from the Basque or Basquan, *i.e.,* mountainous provinces, whose shores are washed by its waters. The **Strait of Gibraltar** honours the reputation of Ben Zeyad Tarik, a Moor-

ish general who effected the invasion of Spain in the
year 712 by obtaining possession of the apparently
impregnable rock which has ever since borne the
name, in consequence, of *Jebel al tarik*, the Mountain
of Tarik. The **Bosphorus** is a Greek term composed of *bous*, an ox, and *porus*, a ford, alluding to the
legend that when Io was transformed into a cow
she forded this strait. The **Dardanelles** derive
their name from the ancient city of Dardanus,
founded by Dardanus, the ancestor of Priam, where
the castle now stands on the Asiatic side.

By the term **Australia** is meant "the South,"
and by **Australasia** " Southern Asia," agreeably to
the Latin *australis*, southern. Previous to its settlement by the British, Australia was known as **New
Holland** owing to its discovery by the Dutch in the
year 1606. The existing name of **New Zealand**
likewise bears testimony to the deep-rooted affection
of the Dutch navigators, and indeed of the Dutch
people generally, for their native country—the word
Zeeland, denoting sea-land, being significant of the
low countries. **Tasmania** was originally known as
Van Dieman's Land, the name bestowed upon it
by Abel Jansen Tasman, who discovered it in 1642,
in compliment to the daughter of the Dutch governor
of Batavia. The change of title was effected in 1853.
The **Society Islands** received their name from
Captain Cook in honour of the Royal Society ; the
Friendly Islands, on account of the friendly disposition of the natives ; and **Christmas Island,**
because he set foot upon it on Christmas Day, 1777.

The naming of the **Sandwich Islands** by Cook conveyed a graceful compliment to Lord Sandwich, First Lord of the Admiralty. The **Philippine Islands,** discovered by Magellan in 1521, were named after Philip II. of Spain ; and the **Caroline Islands** discovered by Lopez de Villalobos in 1543, after Charles V., Emperor of Germany and first King of Spain.

Papua is a Portuguese term for "frizzled," in allusion to the enormous frizzled heads of hair worn by the natives ; **Java** is a native Malay word signifying "the land of nutmegs ; " **Sumatra,** a corruption of *Trimatara,* means "the happy land "; while **Borneo** comes from the Sanskrit *bhurni,* "land." **Japan** is a European modification, brought about through the Portuguese *Gepuen,* of the native *Niphon,* confounded of *ni,* sun, fire, and *pon,* land, literally sun-land, or " land of the rising sun," and signifying "the fountain of light." **Formosa** is Portuguese for "beautiful "; whereas **Ceylon,** rendered in the Portuguese tongue *Selen,* is but part of the original Sanskrit *Sinhala-dwipa,* "the Island of Lions." The **Mauritius**, when colonized by the Dutch, received the name of Maurice, Prince of Orange; and the **Isle of Bourbon,** when settled by the French, that of the Bourbon family. **Madagascar** is properly *Malagasy,* the Island of the Malagese, because the natives belong to the Malay race.

Tierra del Fuego expresses the Spanish for "land of fire." The **Island of Desolation** was so designated by Captain Cook owing to the absence of all

signs of life. **Hanover Island** honours the House
of Hanover; and **Adelaide Island,** the queen of
William IV.; while **Juan Fernandez** (also known
as **Selkirk's Island,** after Alexander Selkirk, its
solitary inhabitant from September, 1704, to February, 1707), perpetuates the name of its discoverer
in the year 1567. The **Ladrone Islands** merited
this designation from the circumstance that when
Magellan touched upon one of the lesser isles of the
group in 1520 the natives stole some of his goods;
whereupon he called the Islands the *Ladrones,* which
is the Spanish for thieves. **Pitcairn's Island** was
discovered by Pitcairn in 1768. **Easter Island** was
so denominated by Jacob Roggevin in consequence
of his visit to its fertile shores on Easter Sunday,
1722; the island having previously been discovered
by Captain Davis in 1686. **Vancouver Island**
preserves the memory of Captain Vancouver, a midshipman under Captain Cook, who discovered it in
1792, while cruising about in search of a river on the
west coast of North America. The **Aleutian Islands**
expresses the Russian for "bald rocks." **Queen
Charlotte Island** was named in compliment to the
queen of George III.; and **Prince of Wales Island,**
after the Prince Regent, afterwards George IV.
Barrow Island, discovered by Captain Penny in
1850, received the name of John Barrow, son of Sir
John Barrow, the eminent statesman; while **Baring
Island,** also discovered by Penny in the course of
the same voyage, received the name of Sir Francis
Baring, First Lord of the Admiralty. The **Parry**

Islands and **Baffin Land** indicate the names of the famous Arctic navigators to whom their discovery was due. **Banks Land** was so called in compliment to Sir Joseph Banks, the eminent naturalist and President of the Royal Society.

Newfoundland is the only territory discovered by Cabot which has been allowed to retain its original name. **Rhode Island,** a corruption of the Danish *rood*, red, signifies Red Island, in allusion to its reddish appearance ; whereas **Long Island** has reference to its long and narrow conformation. The **Bermuda Islands** were discovered by Juan Bermudez in 1522. **San Salvador** means "Holy Saviour." This was the first land sighted by Columbus (October 11, 1492) ; he therefore gave it this name, as a token of thanksgiving. **Jamaica** is a corruption of *Xaymaco*, a native West Indian name signifying "the country abounding in springs." **Cuba** and **Hayti** are also native names, the latter meaning "mountainous country." The Island of **Barbadoes** derived its name from the Latin *barba*, a beard, in allusion to the beard-like streamers of moss always hanging from the branches of the trees. **Dominica** is indicative of the day of its discovery by Columbus, namely, Sunday, November 2, 1493 ; and **Porto Rico** is likewise Spanish for "rich port." When Columbus first sighted the Isle of **Trinidad** he discerned three mountain peaks rising from the sea, thus conveying the impression of three distinct islands ; but on approaching nearer he discovered that they formed one piece of land only ; wherefore he gave the island the name of the Trinity, of which it was so eminently an emblem. But perhaps the most interesting of the West Indies in connection with the subject we are now discussing is **Tobago Island,** so called by Columbus from its fancied resemblance to the *Tobaco,* or inhaling tube of the aborigines, whence the word TOBACCO has been derived. **St. Kitt's Island** is an abbreviation of St. Christopher's Island, so called by Columbus in 1493 after his patron saint.

Ascension Island was discovered by the Portuguese on Ascension Day, 1501; and the **Isle of St. Helena** on the Feast of St. Helena, 1502. **Tristan d'Acunha** received the name of the Portuguese navigator who discovered it in 1651. The **Canary Islands** were originally so called on account of the numerous dogs, as well as of their unusual size(Latin *canis,* a dog), bred here. **Madeira** is a Portuguese term signifying timber ; the inference being that this island was formerly covered by an immense forest. **Majorca** and **Minorca,** literally in accordance with the Latin *major* and *minor,* the Greater and Lesser Island, are denominated also the **Balearic Islands** from the Greek *ballein,* to throw, because their inhabitants were anciently noted slingers. **Corsica** is a Phœnician word denoting " the wooded island " ; **Sardinia** expresses the "land of the Sardonion," a Greek term for a plant indigenous to this island ; **Capri** signifies the "island of goats," agreeably to the Latin *caper,* a he-goat ; **Sicily** received its name from

the *Siculi*, a tribe who settled upon it in early times ;
Malta was anciently *Melita*, " the place of refuge " ;
Candia comes from the Arabic *Khandæ*, " the island
of trenches " ; and **Cyprus** from the Greek *Kupros*,
the name of a herb with which the island abounded ;
while **Rhodes** indicates an " island of roses," in
conformity with the Greek *rhodon*, a rose.

Belleisle is French for " beautiful island " ;
Jersey was originally *Czar's-ey*, meaning " Cæsar's
Island," so called by the Romans in honour of
Julius Cæsar ; the **Isle of Wight** denoted in the
long, long ago the Island of the Wyts, or Jutes ; just
as **Gothland** indicated a settlement of the Goths.
Heligoland expresses the Danish for " holy island
settlement." **Anglesea** is really a corruption of
Anglesey, signifying, in accordance with the suffix *ey*,
the Isle of the Angles [*see* CHELSEA]. The **Isle of
Man** is the modern designation of **Mona Island**,
by which was meant, agreeably to the Celtic *mæn*,
a stone " rocky island." The **Hebrides** were
anciently referred to by Ptolemy as the *Ebudæ*, and
by Pliny as the *Hebudes*, denoting the " Western
Isles " ; the **Orkney Isles** expresses the Gaelic for
the " Isles of Whales," alluding to their situation ;
and the **Shetland Isles,** the Norse for the " Viking
Island," conformably with their native prenomen
Hyalti, a Viking. The term VIKING, by the way,
meaning a pirate, was derived from the *Vik*, or creek,
in which he lay concealed. The name of **Iceland**
needs no comment, further than that, perhaps, the
north and west coasts of the island are frequently

blockaded with ice, which has drifted before the wind
from Greenland. **Spitzbergen** is literal Dutch for
" sharp-pointed mountains," referring to the granite
peaks of the mountains, which are so characteristic
of this group of islands; while **Nova Zembla** presents a strange mixture of the Latin and Slavonic,
literally " new land."

THE MONTHS, AND DAYS OF THE WEEK.

THE titles of the months are modernized forms of those in use among the Romans, namely :— **January,** in honour of Janus, a deity who presided over the beginning of everything; **February,** from the Latin word *febru*, to purify, because the purification of women took place in this month; **March,** after Mars, the God of War; **April,** from *aperio*, to open, this being the month in which the buds shoot forth; **May,** after Maia, the mother of Mercury, to whom sacrifices were offered on the first day of this month; **June,** from Juno, the queen goddess; **July,** the name given to this month by Marc Antony in honour of Julius Cæsar, who was born in it; **August,** named by Augustus Cæsar after himself, because in this month he celebrated three distinct triumphs, reduced Egypt to subjection, and put an end to the civil wars; while **September, October, November,** and **December** literally express the seventh, eighth, ninth, and tenth months of the old Roman Calendar, counted from March, which commenced the year previous to the addition of January and February by Numa in the year 713 B.C.

The Egyptian astronomers were the first to dis-

tinguish the days by names, when, as might have
been expected, they called them after the Sun, the
Moon, and the five planets, viz., Mars, Mercury,
Jupiter, Venus, and Saturn. Of these the two first
and the last survive, but for the rest the names of as
many gods of the Scandinavian mythology have been
substituted. Nowadays, then, we have the following:
—**Sunday,** originally signifying the day upon which
the sun was worshipped ; **Monday,** the day of the
moon ; **Tuesday,** devoted to Tiw, the God of War ;
Wednesday, set apart for the worship of Odin, or
Wodin, the God of Magic and the Inventor of the
Arts ; **Thursday,** the day of Thor, the son of Odin
(or Wodin), and the God of Thunder; **Friday,** allotted
to Frigga, the wife of Odin, and the Goddess of
Marriage ; and **Saturday,** the day of Saturn, one of
the planets of the solar system.

CREEDS, SECTS, AND DENOMINA-
TIONS.

THEISM and **Deism** both express a belief in
God ; the former term being derived from
the Greek *Theos*, God, and the latter from
the Latin, *Deus*, God. The **Theist,** however,
admits the **Theocracy** or Government of God
(Greek *Theos*, God, and *kratein*, to govern) ; the
Deist, on the contrary, maintains that God in the
beginning implanted in all His works certain im-
mutable laws, comprehended by mankind under the
name of the " Laws of Nature," which act of themselves, and are no longer subject to the supervision
of the Creator. **Pantheism** (from the Greek *pan*,
all, everything, and *Theos*, God) is the religion which
rejects a belief in a personal God, but recognizes Him
in all the processes, and works, and glories, and
beauties of Nature, and animated creation. Briefly,
the **Pantheist** holds the doctrine that " God is
everything, and everything is God." The word
Atheism comes from the Greek *Theos*, God, and the
prefix *a*, without. An **Atheist,** therefore, practically
answers to the description given by David in the
opening line of *Psalm* xiv., " The fool hath said in his
heart, There is no God." **Agnosticism** is also

Greek, in accordance with the prefix *a*, without, and *gnomi*, to know. An **Agnostic** is one whose belief is confined to that which he *knows* and sees, and who rejects everything at all beyond his understanding. **Secularism,** derived from the Latin *seculum*, an age, a generation, is the term given to the principles advocated by Messrs. Holyoake in 1846, which professed an entire independence of religion, except so far as it pertains to this life. The **Secularist** aims at promoting the happiness of the community during the present life. His religion is that of this world, without troubling himself about possibilities concerning a life hereafter. Such views are closely allied to those set forth by John Stuart Mill (born 1806, died 1873) under the name of **Utilitarianism,** by which was meant, " the happiness of the greatest number." This term was based upon the Latin *utilitas,* usefulness. **Spiritualism** expresses a belief in the soul's immortality, as opposed to the doctrine of **Materialism,** which contends that the soul, or thinking part of man, is the result of some peculiar organization of matter in the body, with which it must necessarily die. **Rationalism** constitutes the doctrine which accepts the test of Reason and Experience in the pursuit of knowledge, particularly in regard to religious truth, rejecting the gift of Faith, Revelation, and everything connected with the supernatural or miraculous. This was the religion (!) of the French Revolutionists, who set up an actress to be publicly honoured as the " Goddess of Reason " in the

Cathedral of Nôtre Dame on the 10th of November, 1793.

The earliest form of religion on the face of the earth was **Monotheism,** so called from the Greek *monos,* alone, only, and *Theos,* God; therefore signifying a belief in, and the worship of, one Only God. The word **Religion** is derived from the Latin *religare,* to bind. Hence, Religion implies obedience, submission, and an acknowledgment of certain orthodox doctrines regarding our duty to a Supreme Power. **Mosaism,** otherwise **Judaism,** denotes the religion of the Jews as enjoined in the laws of Moses. But even during that favoured period when God manifested Himself in various ways to the children of Israel, Idolatry prevailed. Let us consider what this word **Idolatry** really means. *Idol* is a contraction of the Greek *eidolon,* the diminutive of *eidos,* a figure, an image, or that which is seen, derived from the verb *eidein,* to see; while **Idolater** is made up of the two Greek words, *eidolon,* and *latres,* one who pays homage, a worshipper. An Idolater, therefore, is a worshipper of images, or that which he sees. The Israelites, who prostrated themselves before the Golden Calf, were strictly Idolaters; so were the Egyptians, who worshipped the sun, the moon, the ox, the dog, the cat, the ibis, and the ichneumon; but the Greeks and Romans were scarcely Idolaters, because the mythological deities they worshipped were unseen—as unseen as is the True God Himself. Neither were they **Pagans,** which term, from the Latin *paganus,* a countryman, a peasant, based upon *pagus*, a country, a district, has nothing whatever to do with religion. The Greeks and Romans were, in fact, **Polytheists,** and their religion was **Polytheism,** signifying, in accordance with the Greek *polus*, many, and *Theos*, God, a belief in more gods than one. The more general description of the religion of the ancients is comprised in the term **Mythology,** written in the Greek *muthologia*, from *muthos*, a fable, and *logos*, a discourse.

Alluding to the **Fire Worshippers** of the East, who fall prostrate in adoration of the sun, it should be noted that these do not actually worship the sun, but God, whom they believe to reside in it. This Sun or Fire Worship, the religion of the **Parsees,** otherwise denominated **Zoroastrianism**, was introduced into Persia by Zoroaster about five hundred years before the Christian era. In short, the Parsees are the descendants of those who, in Persia, adhered to the Zoroastrian religion after the Moslem or Mahommedan conquest of their country, whence they were at length driven by Moslem persecution to migrate to India. The **Brahmins** are the priests or higher caste of the Hindoos, who, like the Burmese, the inhabitants of the adjacent country, **Burmah,** claim to be descended from *Brahma*, the supreme deity of the Hindoo religion. The **Buddhists** are the followers of Buddha, a Hindoo sage who founded the doctrine of **Buddhism** in the sixth century B.C. **Mahommedanism** is the religion founded by Mahommed, or Mahomet (born 571, died 632). The term

Koran, or more properly *Al Koran*, " The Koran," which constitutes the Bible of the Mahommedans, is Arabic for a " Reading," a " thing to be read." The native name of the Mahommedan religion is **Islam,** resignation and obedience to God, founded upon the verb *aslama*, to bend, to submit, to sur- render. The Mahommedans of Turkey and Persia usually bear the style of **Mussulmans,** a corruption and the plural of the Arabic *muslim*, rendered into English as **Moslem,** and meaning a true believer, or one who holds the faith of Islam.

Our reference to Mahommedanism having carried us some six hundred years beyond the foundation of **Christianity** by Christ, we must of necessity retrace our steps. Reverting to the Jewish people contemporary with Jesus Christ and His disciples, a certain portion of these styled themselves **Pharisees** because they affected a greater degree of holiness than their neighbours. The name was derived from the Hebrew word *pharash*, separated. The **Nazarenes,** so called after " Jesus of Nazareth," were a sect of semi-converted Jews, who, while believing Christ to be the long-promised Messiah, and that His nature was Divine as well as human, nevertheless continued the rites and ceremonies peculiar to Judaism. The **Gnostics,** otherwise the " Knowers," pursuant to the Greek *gnomi*, to know, were those who tried to accommodate the Scriptures to the speculations of Plato, Pythagoras, and other ancient philosophers; having done which to their own satisfaction they refused all further

5

knowledge on the subject. The **Aquarians** (Latin
aqua, water) insisted upon the use of water in the
place of wine in the Communion. The **Arians**
were the followers of Arius, a presbyter in the
Church of Alexandria, universally regarded as the
first heretic. Soon after his death (in 336), which
was ignominious in the extreme, the Arians re-
nounced their errors, and were readmitted into the
Church; but this gave offence to another section of
the Christians under Lucifer, Bishop of Cagliari,
styling themselves the **Luciferians,** who refused
all communication with the reconverted heretics.
The **Donatists** were the followers of Donatus,
Bishop of Numidia; the **Macedonians,** of Mace-
donius, Patriarch of Constantinople; the **Apolli-
narians,** of Apollinarius, Bishop of Laodicea and
Greek Christian philosopher. These various sects
arose in the fourth century of the Church.

The term **Catholic,** derived from the Greek
Katholos, compounded out of *Kata*, throughout, and
olos, whole, signifies One, Universal. During the
first nine centuries of Christianity the **Catholic
Church** was indeed universal; but at that epoch
it became necessary to distinguish between the
Eastern or Greek Church, and the Western or
Church of Rome, by adding the word " Roman "
to the original Church founded by St. Peter and
perpetuated by his successors the Popes. The
Greek Church, which constitutes the orthodox
religion of Greece, Moldavia, and Russia, differs
principally from the Roman Catholic in regard to

the Papal supremacy, and the doctrine of Holy
Ghost proceeding from the Father and the Son.
The employment of the full title of **Roman
Catholic Church** is at all times necessary in
England when alluding to Christian doctrine in
order to avoid probable confusion with the Estab-
lished Church of this country which retains in its
Creed the designation of " The Holy Catholic
Church." This is because at the Reformation the
Church of England, then styled the **Anglican
Church,** professed to be the Catholic Church
governed by the reigning monarch instead of the
Pope of Rome.

The **Gallican Church** is the so-called Church of
France or Gaul, the ancient name of the country.
Père Hyacinth, its founder, whose church was
opened in Paris February 7, 1870, originally separated from the Church of Rome owing to his dis-
approval of the enforced celibacy of the clergy. The
Lutheran Church of Germany took its name from
Martin Luther (born 1483, died 1546), the monk
who became the pioneer of **Protestantism.** In the
year 1529 the Emperor Charles V. summoned a
Diet at Spiers for the avowed object of enlisting the
aid of the German Princes against the Turks, but
really to devise some means of tranquillizing the
disturbances which had grown out of Luther's
opposition to the Church of Rome, and restoring
the national religion. Against a decree drawn up
at this Diet six princes and the deputies of thirteen
imperial towns offered a vehement *protest*, and ever

afterwards the **Lutherans** were in consequence styled **Protestants.** The first Standard of Faith, according to the doctrines of Luther, is known as **The Augsburg Confession,** because it was presented by Luther and Melancthon to Charles V., during the sitting of the Imperial Diet at Augsburg in the year 1530.

The **Calvinists** were the followers of John Calvin (born 1509, died 1604), the zealous reformer of Switzerland. In due time these also styled themselves Protestants. From Switzerland Protestantism spread into France through the energy of a Genevese Calvinist named Hugh or Hugue, after whom the French Protestants adopted the name of **Huguenots.**

But Luther and Calvin were by no means the earliest of the reformers.

In England the **Wycliffites,** or followers of John Wycliffe (born 1324, died 1387), became known as **Gospellers,** after their leader had completed the translation of the Bible in 1377. Eventually they adopted the title of **Lollards,** in imitation of a sect of German reformers headed by Walter Lollard, a dissolute priest, who turned theologian and was publicly burned for heresy at Cologne in 1322. In France the precursors of the Huguenots were the **Albigenses** of Languedoc, so called because their capital was Albi, and its people were called the Albigeois, early in the twelfth century; and in 1170, the **Waldenses,** inhabiting the wooded districts of Valdois and Piedmont. The latter received their designation in accordance with the German *walden*, forests. The **Camisards,** or wearers of the *Camisè*, a peasant's smock, to conceal their armour, comprised a body of Protestant insurgents who took up arms in the district of the Cevennes after the revocation of the Edict of Nantes by Louis XIV., October 22, 1685. As these always conducted their attacks upon the soldiery under cover of the darkness the term "Camisard" in military parlance soon came to imply a night attack. The Protestants of Bohemia were styled **Hussites,** after John Huss (born 1373, burned 1415); they were also known as **Bethlemites** from the Church of Bethlehem in Prague, in which Huss used to hurl forth his denunciations against the Church of Rome. The **Moravians,** otherwise **The United Brethren,** who were driven by persecutions from Moravia and Bohemia in the last century, claimed to be descendants of the original Hussites.

Having now traced the rise of Protestantism generally, let us at once dispose of the various sects and denominations before confining ourselves to the Established Church and its offshoots.

The **Adamites** were the fanatical followers of one Picard, in Bohemia, self-styled "Adam, Son of God," who, about the year 1400, proposed to reduce mankind to a state of primitive innocence and enjoyment. No clothes were worn, wives were held in common, and many other violations of Nature were committed ere they finally disappeared from the face of the earth. A similar sect were the **Libertines,** in Holland.

These contended that nothing could be regarded as sinful in a community where each was at full liberty to act up to his natural dictates and passions. The **Jansenists** favoured the doctrines of Jansenius, Bishop of Ypres, in France (born 1585, died 1638). For a long period these maintained an open warfare with the **Jesuists,** properly, soldiers of the " Society of Jesus " [*see* RELIGIOUS ORDERS], until they were finally put down by Pope Clement in 1705. The **Gabrielites** were a sect of Anabaptists of Germany in the sixteenth century, named after Gabriel Scherling, their founder. The **Labadists** were a sect of Protestant ascetics of the seventeenth century who conformed to the rules laid down by Jean Labadie, of Bourg, in Germany. The **Socinians,** a sect corresponding to the modern **Unitarians,** owed their existence to Lælius Socinus, an Italian theologian in 1546. The anti-Calvinists of Holland were styled **Arminians,** after the Latinized name (Jacobus Arminius) of their leader, James Harmensen (born 1560, died 1609). The **New Christians** comprised a number of Portuguese Jews in the fifteenth century, who, although they consented to be baptized under compulsion, still practised the Mosaic rites and ceremonies in secret. The **Old Catholics** of Germany are the followers of the late Dr. Döllinger, of Munich (born 1799, died 1890), who refused to accept the dogma of the infallability of the Pope promulgated July 18, 1870.

In our own country the **Scotists** were those who adopted the opinions of John Duns Scotus (born

1272, died 1308), concerning the doctrines of the Immaculate Conception, in opposition to the **Thomists,** or followers of St. Thomas Aquinas (born 1227, died 1274), who denied that the Virgin was conceived without sin. The **Sabbatarians,** known also as the **Seventh Day Baptists,** founded by Brabourne, a clergyman who, about the year 1628, maintained that the seventh day was the real Sabbath as ordained at the beginning. The **Fifth Monarchy Men,** who came into existence during the reign of Charles I., believed in the early coming of Jesus Christ to re-establish the four great monarchies of the ancient world, viz., the Assyrian, Persian, Macedonian, and Roman, contemporaneously with the fifth, the Millennium. The **Muggletonians** were the followers of one Ludovic Muggleton, a journeyman tailor, who set himself up as a prophet in 1651. The **Society of Friends** originally styled themselves **Seekers,** because they sought the truth after the manner of Nicodemus, the Jewish ruler, as narrated in *St. John* iii. 1–21. They were first designated **Quakers** by Justice Bennet of Derby, in 1650, in consequence of George Fox, the founder, having admonished him and all present to quake on hearing the Word of the Lord. The Seekers came into existence in 1646. The **White Quakers,** who seceded from the main body about 1840, are distinguished by their white clothing. The original sect of the **Shakers,** first heard of in the time of Charles I., received its name from the convulsive movements indulged in by its members as part of their peculiar form of

worship. The modern sect sprang from a body of
expelled Quakers, headed by James Wardley, in
1747. They emigrated to America in May, 1772,
and formed a permanent settlement near Albany,
New York, two years afterwards. The **Mormons**
derived their designation from " The Book of
Mormon," claimed to be a lost portion of the Bible
written by the angel Mormon, the last of the Hebrew
line of prophets, and found inscribed in Egyptian
characters upon plates of gold by Joseph Smith, the
founder of the sect, in the year 1827. This work
was really written by the Rev. Solomon Spalding,
who died in 1816. Joseph Smith died in 1844. The
Peculiar People are so styled because they believe
in the efficacy of prayer on the part of their elders,
and the anointing with oil in the name of the Lord
for the cure of sickness as set forth in *James* v. 14.
This sect was first heard of in London in 1838.
The **Faith Healers,** or those who uphold the
doctrine of Healing by Faith, lately sprung up in
our midst, may be regarded as an offshoot of the
Peculiar People. The **Irvingites** are the followers
of Edward Irving, a Scottish divine (born 1792, died
1834), who maintained that Christ was liable to
commit sin in common with the rest of mankind.
The **Humanitarians** incline to the same belief.
The **Sacramentarians** are those who deny the
Real Presence in the Holy Eucharist: the Calvinists
were originally known by this title. The **Plymouth
Brethren** first appeared at Plymouth about the
year 1830; they so style themselves because they

confess Christ as a fraternal community and do not recognize any order of priesthood. The **Perfectionists** of North America are so called owing to their rejection of civil laws, on the plea that the guidance of the Holy Spirit suffices for all earthly as well as spiritual affairs. Another body of coreligionists peculiar to North America are the **Hopkinsians,** named after Samuel Hopkins, of Connecticut, their founder. The doctrines which they hold are mainly Calvinistic.

The **Scottish Covenanters** were those who subscribed to a solemn league or covenant to stand by each other in opposition to the religious and political measures of Charles I. This occurred in 1638. In less than ten years afterwards the Covenanters, having increased in numbers and power, assumed the entire direction of their own ecclesiastical affairs and styled themselves **Presbyterians,** a term derived from the Greek *presbuteros*, an elder, because they contended that the government of the Church as set forth in the New Testament was by presbyters, equal in office, power, and order. The national Church of Scotland, therefore, when at length it was recognized by the English Parliament, bore the title of the **Scottish Presbyterian Church.** It was, however, not long before dissensions became rife. The strictest body of the Presbyterians adopted the style of **Cameronians,** after the name of their leader, Archibald Cameron, who was executed in 1688 on account of his religious opinions; while an equally numerous

body, headed by John Macmillan, became known as
Macmillanites, and also as **The Reformed
Presbytery.** A much later sect was that founded
in 1841 by James Morison, under the designation
of the **Morisonians.** But the most alarming split
in the Presbyterian Church took place May 18, 1843,
when Dr. Chalmers, with a large following, established a separate community, entitled **The Free
Church of Scotland.**

The **Puritans** of England were to the Established
Church what the Pharisees were to the Jews. And
not only did these Puritans profess a greater purity
of doctrine, of morals, and of living, than their
neighbours, but they embraced the earliest opportunity of separating themselves from the Church of
England altogether. They were, in fact, the first of
the Dissenters. On August 24, 1662, which date
witnessed the secession of nearly two thousand
ministers from the Church of England through their
non-compliance with the " Act of Uniformity," the
Puritans joined forces with the latter, and the
combined body assumed the name of **Noncon-
formists.** The Protestants were, consequently,
divided into two great parties—the **Conformists,** or
those who conformed to the requirements laid down
in the " Act of Conformity," and the **Nonconfor-
mists.** The latter have in more recent times borne
the name of **Dissenters,** because they dissent from
the Established Church. The **Sectarians** are
Dissenters who attach themselves to one or other of
the numerous sects and denominations which exist

outside the Church of England. The **Congrega-tionalists** and the **Independents** are one and the same. They maintain that each congregation is an independent religious community entitled to exercise the right of appointing its own ministers and managing its own affairs. These tenets were first publicly advanced by Robert Brown, a violent opponent of the Established Church, in Rutlandshire, as early as the year 1585. The **Unitarians** are the modern **Socinians** already alluded to. They are opposed to the doctrine of the Trinity; and, consequently, to the **Trinitarians.** The **Baptists** not only reject infant baptism, but hold that the adult subject should be baptized after the manner in which Christ was baptized by St. John. On this account the original Baptists, who arose about 1521, received the name of **Anabaptists,** because, having been already baptized during infancy, they of necessity went through the ceremony a second time on arriving at full age. The prefix *ana* is Greek, signifying twice. The followers of John Wesley (born 1703, died 1791) and his brother, Charles Wesley (born 1708, died 1788), were styled **Methodists,** owing to the methodical strictness of their lives and religious exercises. They were also denominated **Wesleyans,** or **Wesleyan Methodists,** in contradistinction to the **Primitive Methodists,** or **Ranters,** who separated from the original sect under Hugh Bourne, in 1810, and retained the style of open-air preaching peculiar to John Wesley in his early itinerant days.

The terms " High Church " and " Low Church "
first came into prominence during the reign of
Queen Anne. Nowadays, as then, that section is
styled **High Church** which regards the Church of
England as the only ark of salvation, while the
less apprehensive and more moderate section is
called **Low Church.** Those who take a still more
liberal and comprehensive view of orthodox doctrine belong to what is known as the **Broad
Church,** which is but another name for **Latitu-
dinarianism,** as originally professed by a number
of divines opposed alike to the Puritans and the
High Church party in the time of Charles I. On
the other hand, the **Ritualists** comprise the extreme
High Church party who are anxious to return to
the ritual of public worship in vogue during the
reign of Edward VI. Prior to 1866, in which year
the term arose, these High Churchmen bore the
name of **Puseyites,** because they agreed with the
views set forth by Dr. Pusey in his celebrated
" Tracts for the Times," published at Oxford
between 1833 and 1841. Those scholars who
assisted Dr. Pusey in the composition of these
Oxford Tracts, as they were called, as well as the
public at large who believed in their teaching, were
styled **Tractarians;** while the great Roman Catholic
revival that took place in the Church of England at
this period universally bore, and still bears, the name
of the **Oxford Movement.**

TAVERN SIGNS.

HOTEL is a French term, derived from *hostil*, a lordly house, a palace. The designation **Public House,** signifying a house of public resort for refreshment and conviviality, is a modern substitute for **Tavern,** derived from the Latin *taberna*, a hut, a wooden booth; frequently also for **Inn,** or rather, as originally written, *Inne*, which expressed the Anglo-Saxon for a mansion. And here we may at once observe that by far the majority of our mediæval inns and **Hostelries** [*see* HOTEL] grew out of the mansions of the nobility during the prolonged absence of their owners. At such times the privilege of utilizing the mansion for his own profit naturally fell to the family's most trustworthy dependent, viz., the head gamekeeper, whose green costume gave existence to the sign of **The Green Man,** when, after quitting the family's service, he set up an inn on his own account either in connection with his own cottage or abutting on the public highway. Nevertheless, this sign had nothing in common with that of the **The Green Man and Still,** expressive of a herbalist bringing his herbs to a distillery, and which was doubtless the sign of a herbalist turned innkeeper.

As the family arms always occupied a prominent position on the front of the mansion these soon became known far and wide, though scarcely in accordance with their full heraldic significance. Briefly, the most conspicuous object in them sufficed to impress itself upon the minds of travellers as the distinguishing sign of the establishment; so that, instead of speaking of *lions gules* and *lions azure*, &c., they simplified matters by referring to red and blue lions, &c. Such was the origin, then, of **The Red Lion, The Blue Lion,** and many another familiar sign of this character. Moreover, as a variation of the same device entered into the arms of different families, it happened that the most conspicuous object in them became popular in different parts of the country at the same time. Another fruitful source of the rapid multiplication of a particular sign throughout the same county, and even upon the same estate, was the fact that as often as a retired dependent of a nobleman's family turned innkeeper, he was pretty certain to name his establishment in accordance with the popular description of the original inn or mansion. If it chanced, however, that that sign had already been appropriated by another innkeeper in the immediate vicinity, the full cognizance of the ground landlord was adopted. Thus, in the Midland Counties there is no sign so common as **The Bear and Ragged Staff,** which was the cognizance of the Earl of Warwick, the King Maker. Similarly, **The Boar's Head** was the cognizance of the Gordons; **The Black Bull,**

that of the House of Clare ; and **The Talbot,** that
of the House of Shrewsbury. Another oft-to-be-met-
with sign is **The Chequers,** which comprised the
arms of the Earls of Fitzwarren who, in the time of
the Plantagenets, held the right of granting the
vintners their licences. Later in our history the
same cognizance was adopted by the Stuarts. As
every one is aware, **The Red Rose** was the recognized badge of the Lancastrians, and **The White
Rose** that of the Yorkists. It may be assumed
that these two signs were naturally more popular
throughout the country at large during the **Wars
of the Roses** than at any subsequent period.
During that turbulent period of English history,
too, the devices of the several adherents of the rival
houses were not unfrequently chosen in commemoration of a particular event ; as, for example, after
the Battle of Barnet, when **The Star,** the badge of
the Earl of Oxford who decided the fate of that day,
sprang up as an inn-sign in all directions, except, of
course, upon Yorkist ground.

Where the innkeeper was not bound by any ties
of gratitude or regard to the ground landlord he
evinced his loyalty to the reigning monarch by
adopting a portion of the royal arms. As examples
of this class :—**The White Swan** was the badge of
Edward III. and of Henry IV. ; **The White Swan
and Antelope,** of Henry V. ; **The White Hart,**
and **The Sun,** both of Richard II. ; **The White
Lion,** of Edward IV. as Earl of March, and **The
Three Suns,** of Edward IV. as King of England ;

The Eagle, of Queen Mary; **The Blue Boar,** of Richard III.; **The Red Dragon,** that of Henry VII., chosen for his standard after the Battle of Bosworth Field, and **The Greyhound,** his original badge as King. **The Rose** is the symbol of England, just as **The Thistle** stands for Scotland, **The Shamrock** for Ireland, and **The Leek** for Wales. A very general expression of loyalty, again, was conveyed in the sign of **The Crown,** which, by the way, was shrewdly complimentary to the reigning house without offering offence to the partisans of a rival claimant to the throne. The **Rose and Crown** had reference originally to the union of the red and white roses in the House of Tudor by the marriage of Henry VII. with Elizabeth, the daughter of Edward IV., in the year 1486; **The Crown and Sceptre** must have originated in the mind of one who had been witness to the elaborate ceremonial peculiar to a coronation; while the **The Crown and Anchor** signified the reliance which was placed in the exalted person that wore the crown.

If, on the other hand, our mediæval innkeeper chose to flatter the ground landlord without actually adopting his cognizance, he invariably named his establishment after his lordship's family title, *e.g.*, **The Earl of March,** in compliment to the Duke of Richmond, or else set up some such sign as **The Hare and Hounds, The Tally Ho! The Fox in the Hole,** &c., in allusion to the sporting tastes of his patron. At times he even went so far as to enter into the religious enthusiasm of the latter by exhibiting a preference for **The Angel** or **The Salutation,** both referring to the Annunciation of the Virgin; **The Three Kings,** meaning the Magi who presented themselves to the Infant at Bethlehem; or **The Cross Keys,** the symbol of St. Peter, and the badge of the Archbishop of York. The sign of **The Mitre** was generally adopted by an innkeeper whose establishment stood in the vicinity of a cathedral; consequently, this particular sign abounds in cities, but is rarely to be met with in the rural districts.

During the period of the Holy Wars, if the innkeeper did not content himself with the sign of **The Turk's Head** or **The Saracen's Head,** that of **The Golden Cross,** which was the ensign carried by the Crusaders, was usually chosen. The modern sign of **The Half-Moon** originated in the crescent, the ensign of the Infidel. The signs of **The Swan, The Pheasant,** and **The Peacock** arose in the days of knight-errantry, when every knight selected one of these birds as an emblem of chivalry, and exerted a pride in the association. For example, one of the principal characters in the " Niebelungen Lied " is called " The Knight of the Swan." Then, again, many innkeepers assumed a sign in honour of the patron saint of England, or in commemoration of his combat with the dragon, viz., **The St. George, The St. George and Dragon, The George and Dragon, The Green Dragon,** &c. **The George,** a common sign enough in our own day—it would be difficult to name a town that has not its " George "

in the High Street—was originally connected with
the dragon too; but at the commencement of the
Hanoverian succession the heraldic device was
painted out altogether, and the words THE GEORGE
were put up in its place. The like observation
applies to all such signs as **The King's Arms,
The Queen's Arms, The Freemasons' Arms,
The Coachmakers' Arms, The Saddlers' Arms,
The Carpenters' Arms,** &c., nowadays identified
by name only, instead of their distinctive badge or
crest. We must not omit to mention also that,
since the especial function of tavern and other signs
was to call attention to the character of an establishment in days when the people were unable
to read, and when, therefore, the display of the
owner's name or of the name of the house
would have been useless, the misapprehension
of the painted device was of common occurrence.
Hence the corruption of many signs from their
original meaning.

Perhaps the most glaring instance of this kind
originated in the sign of **The Garter,** or the insignia
of the Order of the Garter represented in its proper
position on a leg (whence we have the intelligible
sign of **The Star and Garter**); yet the vulgar
mind quite failed to grasp the idea, with a result
that a house exhibiting this sign was invariably
referred to as **The Leg and Star.** Corruptions
of a different character are of later date, when the
name of the house instead of the device began to
make its appearance on an innkeeper's signboard.

Chief among these are:—**The Cat and Fiddle,** a perversion of "Caton le Fidele," in honour of Caton, the faithful Governor of Calais; **The Bag o' Nails,** of "The Bacchanals," in reference to Pan and the Satyrs; **The Goat and Compasses,** of the Puritan motto "God encompass us"; **The Iron Devil,** of "The Hirondelle," or swallow; **The Bull and Mouth,** and **The Bull and Gate,** of "The Boulogne Mouth" and "The Boulogne Gate," in compliment to Henry VIII., who effected the siege of Boulogne and its harbour in 1544; **The Lion and Key,** of "The Lion on the Quay," meaning a house bearing the sign of *The Lion,* and situated by the water-side, in order to distinguish it from other *Lions* in the same port; **The Cat and Wheel,** of "The Catherine Wheel," the instrument of St. Catherine's martyrdom; **The Plume and Feathers,** of "The Plume of Feathers," in allusion to the Prince of Wales; **The Bully Ruffian,** of "The Bellerophon," the vessel on board of which Napoleon surrendered his sword to Captain Maitland after his defeat at Waterloo; and **The Blue Pig,** a mere modification of "The Blue Boar." **The Pig and Whistle** is a very old sign, the term *whistle* being a corruption of "wassail," and *pig,* the Old English for a bowl or cup. Surely there could be no more fitting sign for a tavern than that which suggested the drinking of healths!

The original character of many of our country inns is at once indicated by their signs. Thus, **The Coach and Horses** was clearly, before the introduction of railways, a coaching establishment; while **The Pack Horse** announced the fact that pack-horses were let out on hire. Again, **The Bear** —subject to sundry modifications, such as **The Brown Bear, The Black Bear, The Grizzly Bear**—informed the frequenters of such resorts that bear-baiting might be witnessed on the premises; exactly as, nearer to our own day, **The Dog and Duck** called attention to the popular diversion of duck-hunting by spaniels in a pond. **The Skittles** and **The Bowling Green** indicated a more rational kind of sport. Once more, **The Grapes** conveyed the intelligence that a vinery existed in connection with the establishment; whereas **The Castle,** which constitutes the arms of Spain, **The Globe,** the arms of the King of Portugal, and **The Spread Eagle,** the arms of Germany, told that the wines of those respective countries were to be had there. In the north of England the sign of **The Yorkshire Stingo** is very common, the allusion being to an old beer of particular strength and sharpness for which the county of York has won considerable celebrity.

Among other familiar country inn and tavern signs may be mentioned **The Bell,** referring to the silver bell that formed the prize at races previous to the Restoration ; **The Barley Mow,** denoting the premises where the barley was housed, *mowe* being the Saxon term for "a heap"; and **The Old Hat,** which in the olden time may have been the shop of a hatter rejoicing in the sign of "The Hat," and subsequently converted into a place of refreshment.

Another distinctly tradesmanlike sign is **The Ram and Teazle,** which was originally chosen in com- pliment to the Clothiers' Company ; the lamb with the golden fleece being emblematical of wool, and the teazle, a tool used for raising the nap of the wool when woven into cloth. **The Bricklayers' Arms** merely indicate a house of call for brick- layers ; while **The Cricketers' Arms** derives its title from a neighbouring cricket-ground. The sig- nificance of **The Tankard, The Bottle,** and similar signs, need not detain us. We may, however, state that **The Black Jack** refers to a leathern pitcher for holding beer, which took its name from the defensive breastplate of strong leather formerly worn by horsemen, and known as a *Jacque,* whence the term JACKET has been derived.

Signs that betray a political bias, such as **The Royal Oak, The Boscobel, The Jacobite, The Hanover,** &c., are altogether too numerous to mention. In the early part of the present century, too, the names of political leaders were largely drawn upon as an attraction for tavern signs, as were those also of distinguished naval and military com- manders, and of the battles won by them. **The Canning, The Palmerston, The Nelson, The Wellington, The Marquis of Granby, The Portobello Arms, The Trafalgar, The Water- loo,** and a host of others of the like character, are everywhere to be encountered ; while the old sign of **The Ship** carries us back to the days of Elizabeth, when the circumnavigation of the globe by Sir

Francis Drake was regarded as an exploit that could scarcely be too highly honoured.

Before concluding, let us add a few words of comment upon the signal loyalty of the English people in the times we live in ; for whereas our forefathers were for the most part content to express their loyalty to the throne by the choice of such vague tavern signs as **The King's Head,** or **The Queen's Head,** we of the nineteenth century are not nearly so half-hearted. Not only are **The Victoria, The Prince Albert, The Prince of Wales,** and **The Prince of Wales' Feathers** honoured on every hand in the course of a day's perambulation, but **The Duke of Edinburgh, The Duke of Cambridge, The Duke of Connaught,** and other members of the Royal Family, are similarly memorialized. Perhaps in the future, when the Prince of Wales shall occupy the British Throne, his descendants may also in their turn form the subject of many a tavern sign in our midst.

ROYAL SURNAMES

ALFRED THE GREAT (reigned 871 to 901) fully merited his surname because he expelled the Danes, established a navy, founded schools, and effected the restoration of law and order during one of the most critical periods of early British history. Taking the remainder of the Saxon monarchs in chronological order, we have : — **Edward the Martyr** (975 to 978), treacherously murdered at Corfe Castle; **Ethelred the Unready** (978 to 1016), who, lacking *rede*, or council, fled to Normandy to escape the consequences of a threatened invasion by the Danes; **Edmund Ironsides** (reigned 1016), whose habitual precaution of wearing a complete suit of mail availed him nothing against the fatality of assassination; **Edgar Atheling** (born 1017, died 1120), otherwise "Edgar of Royal Descent"; **Harold Harefoot** (1035 to 1039), swift of foot as a hare; and **Edward the Confessor** (1042 to 1066), so called on account of his holy life. The distinction between a CONFESSOR and a MARTYR in the early days of Christianity was simply this : both made an open confession of their faith, and expressed their readiness to die for it; the former, however, was never called upon to do so, whereas the latter actually suffered martyrdom.

William I. (reigned 1066 to 1087), was styled **The Conqueror** because he defeated the Saxons at the Battle of Hastings, and founded the Norman Dynasty in England. William II. (1087 to 1100), received the name of **Rufus** from his florid complexion; *rufus* being Latin for ruddy. Henry I. (1100 to 1135), was surnamed **Beauclerc,** or good clerk, in recognition of his scholarly attainments. Richard I. (1189 to 1199), styled **Cœur de Leon,** otherwise " The Lion Hearted," is traditionally said to have torn the living heart out of the mouth of a lion to whose fury he was exposed by the Duke of Austria for having killed his son in battle. This extraordinary exploit surpasses the bounds of reason; still there is no doubt that he performed prodigies of valour during the Wars of the Crusades. Another British monarch who rejoiced in a surname of the leonine order was **William the Lion,** King of the Scots (1165 to 1214), so called because he chose a red lion rampant for his crest. It is from this king that the lions distinguished in the Royal Arms of Scotland trace their origin.

King John (reigned 1199 to 1216) received the surname of **Lackland** on account of his improvidence, which at the time of the death of his father (Henry II.) left him entirely without provision. Edward I. (1272 to 1307) was styled **Longshanks** from his spindle legs. The eldest son of Edward III., known as **The Black Prince** (born 1330, died

1376), was not exclusively addicted to the wearing of black armour, as he is usually represented in waxwork shows and picture toy-books; consequently he did not derive his surname from such an association; but, as the historian Froissart informs us, " he received his name by terror of his arms." Seeing that at the age of sixteen he won his knightly spurs at Crecy, and ten years later took the French king prisoner at Poictiers and brought him in triumph to London, the military renown of this young warrior must have been sufficient to command respect from his enemies. **John of Gaunt,** Duke of Lancaster (born 1340, died 1399), took his title from the town of Ghent, in Flanders, where he was born. In like manner his son, Henry IV. (1399 to 1413), was styled **Bolingbroke,** after his native place.

Henry VIII. (reigned 1509 to 1547) was surnamed **Bluff King Hal** on account of his bluff manners; he also received the title of **Defender of the Faith** from Pope Leo X., in recognition of the tract he published against the heresy of Martin Luther. Mary, Queen of Scots (born 1542, died 1587), was known as **The White Queen** because she adopted white mourning for her husband, Lord Darnley. Our own Queen Mary (1547 to 1558) has been handed down to posterity under the opprobrious title of **Bloody Mary,** in consequence of the wholesale burnings of the Protestants under her reign. The religious persecutions of her time admit of no denial, yet they were fully equalled by those brought to light during the reign of her successor, Elizabeth, while they fell

infinitely short of those characterized by the reign
of Henry VIII.   In one sense Elizabeth (1558 to
1603) was appropriately styled **Good Queen Bess,**
inasmuch as she exercised due regard to the interests
of the realm and the welfare of her people.   Her
enemies she speedily removed, but she was just as
ready to bestow honours and rewards upon her
nation's worthies.   Oliver Cromwell was called **The
Lord Protector** (born 1599, died 1658) because he
protected the interests of the Commonwealth.   The
reason why Charles II. (1660 to 1685) was dubbed
The Merry Monarch must be sought in the licen-
tiousness of the times in which he lived.   Much
nearer to our own day, William IV. (1830 to 1837)
was distinguished by the title of **The Sailor King,**
from the circumstance of his having entered the navy
as a midshipman and worked his way upwards until
he attained the rank of Lord High Admiral.

The family name of **Plantagenet,** derived from
the Latin *planta*, a plant, and *genista*, broom, was
originally assumed by Fulke Martel, Earl of Anjou,
the great grandfather of Henry II., in commemoration of the incident, while on his pilgrimage to the
Holy Sepulchre, of having offered himself to be
scourged with the stems of the broom plant by his
two attendants as an atonement for the murder of
the Earl of Brittany.   The **Tudor** Dynasty was
founded by Owen Tudor, a Welsh soldier stationed
at Windsor, who contracted a secret marriage with
Catherine, the widowed queen of Henry V.   The
first of the long line of the **Stuart** sovereigns

(Scottish and English) was Walter, the Lord High Steward of Scotland, whose wife was the daughter of King Robert the Bruce. As this Walter was the sixth member of his family that had held the post of Lord High Steward, he was popularly said to belong to the *Stewards,* until in course of time this word became corrupted into *Stuarts,* and was adopted as a family name.

Charles I., Emperor of Germany (born 742, died 814), was surnamed **Charlemagne,** otherwise Charles the Great. **The She-Wolf of France** was Isabella (born 1290, died 1357), daughter of Philip IV. of France, and queen of Edward II. of England, whom she, in concert with the Earl of Mortimer, her paramour, murdered by thrusting a red-hot iron into his bowels. **Pedro the Cruel,** King of Castille and Leon in 1350, merited his surname owing to his cruel treatment of his two brothers, whom he murdered, and his queen, whom he poisoned. Ivan II., Czar of Russia (reigned 1533 to 1584), was styled **The Terrible** on account of the cruelties he inflicted upon all who offended his autocracy. Frederick I., of Germany (reigned 1152 to 1190), was surnamed **Barbarossa** from his red beard, *barba* being Latin for beard; while for his bombardment of Messina in 1848 Ferdinand, King of Naples, was nicknamed **Bomba.** Philippe, Duc d'Orleans, the father of Louis Philippe, King of France, assumed the name of **Egalité** when he joined the Republican party in 1789. Of a truth, if " Equality " was what this not unworthy

Prince aspired to, he enjoyed it to the full, for he lost his head under the guillotine in common with more than twenty thousand of his fellow-citizens.

NATIONAL NICKNAMES.

BROTHER JONATHAN, the popular nickname of the United States, arose out of the
person of Jonathan Trumbull, the Governor
of Connecticut, whom General Washington never
failed to consult in cases of emergency. "We must
refer the matter to Brother Jonathan!" he was
wont to exclaim when no other officer could offer
any practical suggestion to aid him out of a difficulty; and true enough, "Brother Jonathan" proved
himself in every instance equal to the confidence
reposed in him. Another stock nickname for the
United States is **Uncle Sam.** This originated from
a vulgar misconception of the initial letters "U. S."
(United States) for those of the well-known sobriquet of an official whose business it was to mark
them on all Government property. The numerous
acquaintances of this person understood that the
goods so marked had passed through the hands of
"Uncle Sam," and the joke becoming public it spread
far and wide, until in the end it was considered far
too good to be allowed to drop. The term **Yankee**
finds its origin in the native attempt to pronounce
the word "English," but approaching no nearer
to the sound than *Yengees*, the name bestowed upon

the English colonists by the Indians of Massachusetts, and afterwards given to the New Englanders by the British soldiers during the American War.

The nickname of the typical Englishman, **John Bull,** was derived from Dr. Arbuthnot's satire of this title published in 1721. There was also a real person of the name of John Bull, well known as the composer of " God Save the King "; but he died just a hundred years before Dr. Arbuthnot's performance was heard of. Of a still later date is the national English nickname, **Mrs. Grundy,** which arose out of the passage, " What will Mrs. Grundy say ? " from Thomas Morton's drama, " Speed the Plough," produced in 1798. The proverbial prudishness of the English people in matters affecting art, could scarcely be better expressed than under the style of **The British Matron.** The British soldier is popularly referred to under the general designation of **Tommy Atkins,** because " Thomas Atkins" was a fictitious name that figured in the soldiers' monthly statement of accounts.

The Irish as a nation are invariably alluded to as **Pat** or **Paddy,** being short for Patrick, their most common Christian name, selected in honour of St. Padhrig, or Patrick (born 373, died 466) ; the Scots as **Sandie** or **Sawney,** a contraction of Alexander, their most popular Christian name ; and the Welsh as **Taffy,** a corruption of Davy, and short for David, the name of their Archbishop and Saint (born 490, died 554).

The national nickname of the Chinese is **John**

Chinaman, in imitation of our own characteristic
" John Bull." Even now a Chinaman addresses
every Englishman he meets as " John," which is his
idea of our most popular name. Hence, British
sailors in the Chinese waters from the first returned
the compliment, so to speak, by alluding to each
Celestial with whom they came in contact as " John
Chinaman."

The Chinese are also called **Pigtails,** on account
of their Tartar tonsure and braided *queue.* By the
Indians of North America Europeans are styled
Pale Faces; while the Europeans designate the
Indians **Red Skins,** both terms having reference to
the complexion. The word **Nigger** is a corruption
of **Negro,** derived from *niger,* the Latin for black.
The reason why a negro generally bears the name of
Sambo is because *Zambo* is the native term used to
designate the offspring of a black person and a
mulatto. The word **Mulatto** is Spanish, derived
from the Latin *mulus,* a mule, and signifying a mixed
breed. A Mulatto may be either the offspring of a
negress by a white man, or of a white woman by a
negro.

BIRDS.

THE following owe their names to their characteristic note :—the **Cuck-oo**, the **Pee-wit**, the **Cur-lew**, the **Chick-a-dee**, and the **Whip-poor-will**. The **Trumpeter** of South America is so called on account of its loud, clear, and trumpet-like cry. The word **Nightingale** is a modern form of the Anglo-Saxon *nihtegale*, indicative of a bird that sings by night, agreeably to its component parts, *niht*, night, and *gale*, a songster. The **Night-Jar** bears its name because the sound it emits resembles the whirring of a spinning-wheel. The **Mocking-bird** possesses the power of imitating the notes of other birds; while the **Humming-bird** is remarkable for the humming sound that proceeds from its wings as it speeds through the air.

Several birds are named after the colour or some other characteristic of their plumage. Among these we have the **Greenfinch** and the **Goldfinch**, the term **Finch** from the Anglo-Saxon *finc*, denoting a small singing bird; the **Greenlet** expressing a tiny green bird peculiar to South America; the **Jay**, a corruption of *gai*, its French name, alluding to its gay or showy appearance; the **Blue-bird**, common in the United States, the upper half of which is blue; the **Blackbird,** so called from its sable aspect; the **Starling,** owing to the specks at the extremities of its feathers; the **Flamingo,** of South America and Africa, from its flaming colour; the **Oriole,** an Australian bird of golden-yellow plumage, agreeably to the Latin *aureolus,* golden; and the **Lyre-bird,** also a native of Australia, so denominated on account of the sixteen feathers of the tail which when folded form in appearance a perfect lyre. The British song-bird known as the **Red-poll** receives its name from the tuft of red feathers upon its head; whereas the South African **Secretary-bird** is so called because a tuft of feathers on each side of its head are supposed to resemble quill pens stuck behind the ear. The South American **Birds of Paradise** are indeed a beautiful species, all the colours of the rainbow being represented in their plumage; and the same may be said of the **Love-birds,** so designated from the extraordinary affection which they exhibit towards one another. The **Kingfisher** is regarded as the king of fisher-birds, or those that dive for fish as their prey, by reason of his gay plumage.

The **Lapwing** derives its name from the loud flapping noise made by its wings during flight; the **Wagtail,** from the incessant wagging of its tail; and the **Scissors-tail**—found only in South America—from the peculiar nature of its tail, which, like a pair of scissors, opens and shuts in the course of its rapid passage through the air and so entraps the flies upon which it preys. The **Hangbird** is so called from its habit of suspending its nest from the limb of a tree; the **Weaver-bird,** from the wonderful intertwining of twigs and grass displayed in the construction of its nest; and the **Tailor-bird,** from the skill it displays in constructing its nest by stitching together the leaves of plants.

Among corruptions of the names of birds it will be sufficient to mention the **Widow-bird,** properly the *Whydaw-bird*, after the territory in Africa of which it is a native; the **Martin,** from the Latin *murustenco*, or wall-swallow, shortened into *murten*, and mispronounced *marten;* and the **Muscovy Duck,** which, so far from claiming a Muscovite origin, is merely a *musk duck*, a species somewhat larger than our common duck.

The **Swift** derives its name from its rapid flight; the **Passenger-pigeon,** from its migratory habits; the **Skylark,** from mounting to the sky and singing as it flies; and the **Chaffinch,** from its preference for chaff above every other kind of food. The **Diver** is remarkable for its habit of diving; the **Sandpiper** inhabits the sea-beach; and the **Chimney-swallow** builds his nest in an ordinary house chimney. The **Horn-bill,** the **Boat-bill,** the **Spoon-bill,** and the **Duck-bill** are respectively so named on account of the resemblance of their bills to the articles, and in the last-mentioned case to the bird, indicated; while the **Cross-bill** has its mandibles crossed in opposite directions. The **Pouter-pigeon** is so called from the pouting, or bulging out, of its breast; the **Ring-dove,** from the white ring around its neck; and the

Wryneck, from the curious manner in which it turns its neck over its shoulder when surprised. The **Woodcock** is found in the underwood of a forest, while the **Woodpecker** pecks holes in the bark of trees in search for insects.

Chief among the birds which derive their names from the countries to which they originally belonged are the **Guinea-fowl,** brought from Guinea, West Africa; the **Brahma-fowl,** from the neighbourhood of the Brahmapootra River in India; the **Bantam,** from Bantam in Java; the **Barb,** from Barbary, and the **Turkey,** which, although an American bird, was long believed to have been imported from European Turkey. Another native of North America received its name of the **Baltimore-bird** from the fact that its colours corresponded with those which occurred in the arms of Lord Baltimore, the Governor of Maryland, in which State it principally abounds. The **Canary** was first brought from the Canary Islands in 1500. The **Petrel,** a sea-bird usually associated with storms, expresses the Anglicized form of the Italian *petrillo,* a diminitive of Peter, in allusion to St. Peter walking on the sea, and the frequent appearance of this bird standing as it were on the surface of the water.

RELIGIOUS ORDERS.

STRICTLY speaking, the members of the various Religious Orders, in this country at least, are not **Monks,** but Friars. Only those who live completely isolated from the rest of mankind, as did St. Anthony, are entitled to the former designation, which, in common with the term **Monastery,** comes from the Greek *monos*, alone. Consequently, a Religious House is incorrectly described as a Monastery unless each individual within its walls occupies a separate cell, both by night and by day, and never suffers himself to have the least communion with his neighbour. Failing compliance with such a rule, the term **Convent,** derived from the Latin *con*, together, and *venire*, to come, is more fittingly applicable. This designation, however, is now borne by an institution reserved for a community of **Nuns,** so called from the Italian *nonna*, a grandmother, because they originally comprised only very aged women; albeit it was formerly the custom to speak of Monasteries and Convents without discrimination. An **Abbey** always indicated a Religious House in connection with a Church, as, for example, Westminster Abbey, the abode of the community attached to the West Minster, presided over by an **Abbot,** so styled in accordance with the Syriac and Latin *abba,* a father, or, in the case of a female community, by an **Abbess;** whereas a **Priory** denoted a lesser or branch establishment placed at some distance from the Abbey, and controlled by a **Prior** (or **Prioress**), signifying one who had a prior claim over the rest to the office of Abbot (or Abbess) in the original community.

A **Friar,** on the other hand, is—conformably to the Latin *fratre* and the French *frère,* a brother— what the term implies, viz., one of a brotherhood. In olden times there existed four distinct and power- ful Orders of Friars. These were the **Dominicans,** founded by St. Dominic to preach away the Albi- gensian heresies, also known as the **Black Friars,** on account of their black habits, and in France as the **Jacobins,** because their first convent was situated in the Rue St. Jacques, Paris; the **Fran- ciscans,** or **Grey Friars,** named after St. Francis d'Assissi; the **Carmelites,** or **White Friars** of Mount Carmel; and the **Augustines,** or **Austin Friars,** whose origin is ascribed to St. Augustin or Austin, the first Archbishop of Canterbury, who died in 605. Eventually a fifth Order, styled the **Trinitarians,** or Friars of the Holy Trinity, other- wise the **Crutched Friars,** so called from the cross (Latin *cruciati,* crossed) embroidered on their habit, came into existence.

Referring to the Franciscans, those who con- formed to the austere rules laid down by their founder were denominated **Observant Friars,** while those who, as time wore on, began to live in convents and coveted lands, chapels, and books, received the name of **Conventional Friars.** Out of the Franciscans there have sprung two lesser Orders, so to speak, chiefly distinguished by a slight change in the details appertaining to the habit worn by them. These are the **Capuchins,** so called from the *capuce,* or pointed cowl, that they wear, and the **Cordeliers,** from the knotted cord which encircles their waist in place of a girdle. In effect, however, these two offshoots of the Franciscans are the same, and subject to the like rules, as the parent institution.

Having disposed of the Friars, let us now turn to the Monks properly so called. Originally the sole existing order of monks was that of the **Benedictines** as established by St. Benedict, who introduced the monastic system into Western Europe in the year 529. No less than twelve large Monasteries were raised by him before he died ; but notwithstanding the austere rules which obtained among the Benedictines, these were yet considered too lax by some individual members of the Order, with the result that first one and then another " Reformed Order " sprang into existence, the latest being in each case distinguished for a still more rigorous rule than that of its immediate predecessor. Thus, we now have the **Carthusians,** our English designation for the monks of La Chartreuse near Grenoble, by whom the celebrated liqueur known as **Chartreuse** is prepared ; the **Cistercians,** or monks of Citeau ; and the **Cluniacs,** or monks of Cluny, respectively named after the vicinity of their original monastery in France ; while the **Bernardines** received their title from St. Bernard, who founded the famous Hospice of Mont St. Bernand in the year 962. From the Carthusians, also, there have sprung the **Basilians** founded by St. Basil, and from the Cistercians, the **Trappists,** or monks of La Trappe, originally established in the French district so denominated.

Foremost among the Religious Orders not comprised in any of the brotherhoods cited above are the **Jesuists,** properly styled "The Society of Jesus," an organization founded upon a military basis by St. Ignatius Loyola in 1534, which extends its influence all over the globe. Next in point of importance come the **Servites,** otherwise " The Religious Servants of the Holy Virgin," established by seven Florentine merchants in 1283 ; the **Passionists,** a community of priests solemnly agreed to preach " Jesus Christ and Him crucified," founded by Paul Francis, better known as St. Paul of the Cross, in 1737 ; and the **Redemptorists,** or preachers of the Redemption, also styled the **Liguorians,** after St. Francis Liguori, who originated this Order in 1732. Each of these, except, of course, the lay members of the Jesuists, are professedly Monks ; and yet these are not really Monks, but *Friars,* because they live in community, and at times mingle freely with the people. In short, they are **Missionary Friars.**

PAPER AND PRINTING.

THE word **Paper** comes from the Latin *papyrus*, and Greek *papyros*, the designation of an Egyptian plant from whose reeds the earliest kind of writing material was obtained. **Parchment** is an Anglicized form of the French *parchemin*, from the Greek *pergamenos*, named after the ancient city of Pergamos, in Asia Minor, where the skins of goats were first prepared for writing upon at a time when Ptolemy prohibited the exportation of the papyrus from Egypt.

Hand-paper was originally so called from its watermark, which was that of a hand ; **Pot-Paper,** of a pot ; **Post**-paper, of a post-horn ; **Crown-paper,** of a crown ; and **Foolscap,** of a fool's head with the cap and bells. **India-paper** formerly came from the Far East, whereas **Nepaul-paper** is made in the district of Nepaul, Northern India. **Cap-paper** is so designated because, prior to being used by grocers for wrapping up sugar and other commodities sold by weight, it is folded into a cap-like form. Among papers of a stiffer kind, that are chiefly intended for drawing upon, we have **Elephant,** so called from its large size (28 inches by 23), **Cartridge-paper,** originally manufactured for soldiers' cartridges, and **Bristol-board,** formerly made only at Bristol.

By the term **Folio,** derived from the Latin *folium,* a leaf, is meant a sheet of paper folded but once, thus making two leaves or four pages; a **Quarto** (written 4to), is a sheet folded into quarters or four leaves, making eight pages; an **Octavo** (8vo), so styled in accordance with the Latin *octa,* eight, one folded into eight leaves or sixteen pages; a **Duo-decimo** (12mo), the Latin for "two and ten," one making twelve leaves or twenty-four pages, and so forth.

When Caxton set up the first printing press in this country, in the year 1476, there were many among the vulgar who regarded it as an invention of the devil; and the clergy, no doubt, fostered this idea, foreseeing that in the event of the Bible being distributed to the masses by this means, the way would be thrown open to the production of spurious editions of Sacred Writ, and the perversion of reli-gious doctrine, which up to that period had been free to all who chose to attend daily instruction in the monasteries. Hence, printing was popularly de-scribed as " The Black Art," while the boys who took the sheets off the press, from the fact of gene-rally smearing their faces with ink, came to be known as Imps or Devils. This will explain why a printer's errand-boy still bears the nickname of a **Printer's Devil.**

Our Parliamentary Records, Debates, Reports of Meetings, and Accounts, have received the name of

Hansards because they are printed by the large printing firm established by Luke Hansard in 1752; whereas a **Blue Book** is so called on account of its stiff cover of blue paper. The French Government reports are styled **Yellow Books** for a similar reason. The term **Book** comes from the Danish *bog*, a beech-tree, which abounds in Denmark and whose wood is much used for engraving-blocks. The **Leaf** of a book is in allusion to the ancient custom of writing on the bark of trees; while **Volume** is derived from the Latin *volvo*, I roll, relative to the Egyption papyri, each one of which when rolled up formed a document or volume complete in itself. A storehouse for books is styled a **Library,** in accordance with the Latin *librarium*, a book-case, derived in the first instance from *liber*, a book.

A **Pamphlet** owes its description to Pamphila, a Greek lady who left behind her a kind of commonplace book containing notes, epitomes, and anecdotes. The French equivalent for a pamphlet is a **Brochure,** so called from the verb *brocher*, to stitch, because such a book consists only of a few pages stitched together. The word **Chart** comes from the Latin *charta*, a leaf of paper; a chart, therefore, is not printed on canvas like a map, but on a single sheet of paper. **Map** traces its origin from *mappa*, a Punic word which signified a signal-cloth, also a napkin, because in ancient times military and other landmarks were sketched upon a cloth in the absence of parchment and paper. Nowadays, a book of maps designed for school use is called an **Atlas,** after the fabled King of Mauritania of this name, who was believed by the ancients to support the world on his shoulders. The figure of Atlas with the globe first appeared as a frontispiece to " Mercator's Projections," published about the year 1560.

A **Cartoon,** as we understand the term, is a representation of political significance, usually coloured and printed on stiff paper. To some extent this kind of publication owes its origin to the celebrated ' Cartoons " of Raffaelle, now in the South Kensington Museum, so called because they were drawn upon *cartone,* the Italian for pasteboard. A **Broadside** consists of a large sheet of paper having the matter printed straight across, instead of in columns, so as to admit of being read at one broad view. The reverse side of the sheet is left blank. A **Poster** bears its name from the fact that formerly the sidewalks of London streets, instead of being paved as as now, were distinguished from the centre, or sedan-chair and riding way, by a series of posts ; and upon these theatrical and other announcements were *posted.* In France, the theatre bills are exhibited upon the lamp-posts on the Boulevards in a similar manner. In conclusion, the distinction between BOOK-SELLERS and STATIONERS was originally this : the former were itinerant sellers of books, like hawkers, and pedlars, whereas the latter had stalls at the corners of streets or in open market ; and as the *stationarii,* or stationary booksellers, were enabled to display a more varied stock than the itinerants who carried books only, such articles as writing-paper, pens, ink, and other materials in course of time received the name of **Stationery.**

POLITICAL NICKNAMES.

THE utmost difficulty exists in reconciling the various opinions expressed by different authors concerning the origin of the terms **Whig** and **Tory.** And yet, if we but consider the reasons why these nicknames were first bestowed upon the two great political factions of this country during the reign of Charles II., we may possibly attain a much-desired end. In the year 1648 (*temp* Charles I.) there occurred a rising, or sally, of the peasantry inhabiting the south-western districts of Scotland against the Royalists. This was known as the **Whigamore Raid,** the term *whigamore* being applied to the teamsters and ploughmen of those parts because they used the twin-syllabic cry of " Whi-gam ! " to drive their horses. When, therefore, in the early days of the Restoration, the ultra-Protestant party opposed certain measures of the Government, the Catholics reproached them with favouring the fanatical opinions of the Scottish Covenanters and Whigamores, and styled them **Whigs.** In return the Protestants bestowed upon their opponents the nickname of **Tories,** the familiar designation of a band of Irish out-laws who sought refuge in the bog districts of

Ireland. The word Tory, or rather *Toree*, is Irish, signifying a robber. From that time down to the present **Toryism** has been considered to denote a steadfast adherence to constitutional principles and the maintenance of royalty and the peerage, as opposed to the progressive and more *liberal* views appertaining to **Whiggism,** which advocates constitutional reform and a moderate extension of democratical powers. The word **Liberal** was first employed by Lord Byron and his friends as the title of a periodical intended to set forth the political aims of the advanced Whig party in 1828. The term **Conservative** (derived from the Latin *con,* together, and *servare,* to keep, to preserve) first appeared in an article in *The Quarterly Review,* January, 1830, and was permanently adopted by the Tory party on the passing of the Reform Bill two years afterwards. The still more advanced section of the Whig party which came into prominence in 1816 were styled **Radicals, or Radical Reformers,** from their desire to institute a *thorough* reformation in the national policy. In our own day the Radicals and the Democrats may be set down as one and the same party ; while the **Socialists** eminently carry out the principles of the primitive Radicals of the time of Charles I., who styled themselves **Levellers** because they strove to reduce society to a common level The word **Democrat** is derived from the Greek *demos,* people, and *kratein,* to govern ; therefore denoting one who upholds the principle of government by the people themselves, and diametrically opposed to an **Aristocracy** (Greek, *aristos*, best, and *kratein*, to govern), or government by the bravest and best. These terms were first brought into notice by the French Revolutionists of 1790.

Adverting to the protracted struggle between the **Royalists** under Charles I. and the **Parliamentarians** under the Cromwellian Parliament, no two nicknames could have been more suggestive of their origin than those respectively of the **Cavaliers** and the **Roundheads.** The latter arose out of the Puritan fashion of cropping the hair close round the head, the former from the cavalier manner in which a number of gentlemen offered themselves as a permanent escort to the King after he had been subjected to insult in December, 1641. The word Cavalier is synonymous with the French *chevalier*, a mounted knight, from *cheval*, a horse, derived from the Latin *caballus*, and the Greek *kaballes*, an inferior horse.

The Protestants in Ireland received the name of **Orangemen** owing to their adherence to William III., Prince of Orange, while the Roman Catholics were styled **Jacobites** from their adhesion to James II., *Jacobus* being the Latin form of the King's name. The **Peep o' Day Boys** were so called because they broke into the houses of the people at dawn of day in quest of arms ; and the **White Boys,** from the white smocks they wore over their clothing. The depredations of both these insurgents were finally put an end to by the Insurrection Acts, passed in 1786–7. The secret brotherhood of the **Fenians,** organized for the overthrow of the English rule in Ireland, derived its name from Fiona Mac Cumhal, better known as Fingal, after whom FINGAL'S CAVE is designated. The correct interpretation of the Gaelic word *Fenian* is "a hunter." Another secret society of quite recent origin is that of the **Irish Invincibles,** established, as was publicly stated by Carey the Informer, for the "making of history by killing tyrants." Their title is due to the boast that they defy extermination. The **Ribbonmen** take their name from the distinctive badge which they wear. **Emergency Men** are the more active members of the Irish Defence Association. The **Separists** and the **Parnellites** are one and the same, sworn to support the measures of Mr. Parnell and the Irish National Party in promoting Home Rule for Ireland. The now familiar word **Boycotting,** in connection with Irish affairs, arose out of the troubles experienced by Captain Boycott, of Lough Mask Farm, near Ballinrobe, County Mayo, the land agent of Lord Erne. His house was besieged, his labourers were threatened, his crops remained ungathered, and tradesmen refused to supply him with goods. This occurred on the 11th and 12th of November, 1880, after which the military was despatched to his aid, and a "Boycott Fund" subscribed for his benefit. The expression "to boycott" a man practically means to place him beyond the pale of civilization.

The lowest order of the French Revolutionists

were denominated **Sansculottes,** literally, " without breeches," because they rejected those very service-able articles of attire as being emblematical of the aristocracy. The same term was also applied to the Republican leaders as a reproach for the negligence of their dress; but after a time they themselves adopted the title with pride. The **Red Republicans** were so called for a two-fold reason. In the first place, they did not hesitate to steep their hands in human blood to accomplish their political aims; and, secondly, they wore the red cap, symbolical of Liberty from the days of the Romans downwards. The two antagonistic parties of the Revolution were styled **The Mountain** and **The Plain** for the reason that the former sat upon the most elevated benches in the Hall of Assembly, while the latter occupied the ground floor. The Plain was for the most part composed of the **Girondists,** or deputies from the Department of the Gironde.

The **Hats** and the **Caps** were the two great political factions in Sweden, so called on account of the French *chapeaux* worn by the partisans of the French interest on the one side, and the Russian caps worn by the partisans of the Russian interest on the other. *Apropos* of Russia, the word **Nihilist** (derived from the Latin *nihil,* nothing), originally denoted a social rather than a political party opposed to the tyranny of custom. Its significance is well expressed by Turgeneff, who first introduced it in his novel " Fathers and Sons," published in 1862 :—" A Nihilist is a man who bows before no

8

authority, who accepts no principle without examination, no matter what credit the principle has." At the present day a Nihilist is a revolutionary Socialist of the most pronounced degree.

The Italian **Carbonari,** being the plural of *carbonaro,* a coal-man, a charcoal-burner, who first came into notice in 1820, assumed their designation from the fact of their meetings being originally held in the huts of the charcoal-burners, and because they held charcoal to be the symbol of purification.   The **Black Cloaks** were the upper classes of Naples, distinguished by the colour and quality of their cloaks from the **Lazzari,** or beggars.   Regarded as a political party, the Neapolitan Black Cloaks no longer exist ; but the **Lazzaroni,** so called from the Hospital of St. Lazarus, which serves for their refuge, are still to be met with in all quarters of the city.   Then, again, we must not omit mention of the **Guelphs** and the **Ghibellines,** names of two powerful families whose rival partisanship of the Papal and the Imperial supremacy in Italy threatened the peace of Europe during the long period embraced between the years 1250 and 1500.

The word **Federal** comes from the Latin *fœdus,* a league or compact.   A federal form of government is one under which a number of States, while retaining their individual institutions and autonomy, unite together for purposes of defence and for a larger national existence, delegating to a representative national government certain specified powers.   The most noteworthy examples in history of this form of government are the Achaean League, the Swiss Republic, and the United States of America. In the early history of the United States the term "Federal" was applied to that one of the two great political parties which was supposed to be more particularly in sympathy with English standards and to favour an English alliance, and which desired a strong central government. Their opponents, who pre- ferred a French alliance, and who opposed a strong central government, were then termed "Repub- licans."

About 1830 the "Federals" became **Whigs,** and in 1856 they assumed the name of **Republicans** (from *res publica,* the State), the States-rights party having in the meantime taken the name of "Demo- crats" (from *demos,* the people). During the civil war of 1861–1865 the Northerners were all termed "Federals" (or by their opponents "Yankees" or "Yanks"), while the Southerners had taken the name of **Confederates,** because their Constitution instituted a weaker central government and favoured the independent action of the several States.

The Southerners were also given the nickname of "Corn-feds," in allusion to the chief article of their diet. The term **Yankee** above alluded to dates back to the seventeenth century, and is a modifica- tion of the name "Yengees," an attempt by the Massachusetts Indians to pronounce the name "English."

By the residents of the Northern States, the term is limited to the inhabitants of the six States of New

England. During the civil war of 1861–1865, the
members of a political faction in the North received
the name of **Copperheads,** because they were regarded as secret foes to the national cause. The
allusion was to the poisonous copperhead serpent,
which gives no warning of its approach. The
Know-nothings were a secret political party in
the United States (1848–1860), whose chief aim was
the checking of foreign immigration and the political
influence of foreigners by the repeal of the Naturaliza-
tion Laws, and the reserving of public appointments
for native-born Americans. The answer given by
its members to all questions about the party organization was, " I don't know."

The **Tammany Ring** was the name used to
designate an organization among certain officials
and their backers in the city of New York in 1870–
1871, who succeeded for a time in enriching themselves at the expense of the city. The ring was
overthrown in 1871, and its leaders imprisoned or
banished. The name of the ring arose from Tammany Hall, the headquarters of a society originally
founded (in 1805) for benevolent purposes, but which
had become a political power, and which is again
(1892) controlling the government of New York.

The term **Mugwump** first came into political use
in 1884. It was then applied to voters who had
been " Republicans," but who, on various grounds,
preferred the Democratic candidate Cleveland to the
Republican Blaine, and who succeeded in electing
the former. It has since been given generally to

citizens, who, while actively interested in politics, refuse to be bound closely by party ties, considering causes such as free trade, civil service reform, honest money, &c., as more important than party labels or party success. The name " Mugwump " is said to be derived from an Indian word signifying "wise chief."

The **Chartists** constituted an enormous body of the people of this country who, soon after the passing of the Reform Bill in 1832, loudly clamoured for "The People's Charter," of which the six principal points were these :—Universal Suffrage, Vote by Ballot, Annual Parliaments, Payment of the Members, Abolition of the Property Qualification, and the Equalization of Electorial Rights. William Lovett, the author of this document, died in August, 1877. The English war party, who sided with the Turks in the Russo-Turkish struggle of 1878 received the nickname of **Jingoes, or The Jingo Party,** from the chorus of Macdermott's famous music-hall song, commencing—

> "We don't want to fight, but, *by Jingo*, if we do !"

" Jingo " is a corruption of *Jainko*, the Basque term for God. Hence the expression, " By Jingo ! " is properly a direct appeal to the Deity. A **Protectionist** is one who advocates the protection of home-produce and manufactures against foreign competition by the imposition of import duties.

FLOWERS.

The name of **Forget-me-not** originated in the following legend:—A German knight and his lady were walking on the bank of the Danube, when the fair one saw a beautiful tuft of *Myosotis palustris* growing in the water, and expressed a wish to have it. With chivalrous alacrity the knight at once plunged into the river and gathered his prize; but before he could regain the steep and slippery bank, encumbered as he was by his heavy armour, he was drawn by the treacherous eddy into a deep pool. Finding he could not save himself, he threw the flowers ashore to his mistress as he sank, and uttered with his last breath the words "*Vergess mein nicht!*" ("Forget-me-not!") Hence this flower has come to be universally regarded as the emblem of fidelity.

Mignonette, the diminutive of *Mignon*, the French for "darling," is so called on account of its delicate fragrance. The **Carnation** owes its name to the Latin *caro*, flesh, in relation to its colour. **Geranium** comes from the Greek and Latin *geranos*, a crane; this genus of plants having a beak-like torus, or receptacle. It is also known as **Crane's-bill** for the same reason. **Pansy** is an Anglicized form of

the French *pensée,* "thoughts," this being the senti-
ment expressed by the flower.

The **Camellia** was named after G. J. Camelli,
the German botanist and missionary (died 1690), by
whom it was introduced into Europe from the East ;
the **Dahlia,** after Andrew Dahl, the Swedish botanist,
who discovered it in Mexico in 1784; and the **Fuchsia,**
after Leonard Fuchs, who brought it from Mexico
about the year 1542. The **Victoria Regia** was so
called because it was introduced into this country
from British Guiana soon after the accession of
Queen Victoria. The **Adonis** is said to have
sprung out of the blood of Adonis, the beautiful
youth who was gored to death by a boar; and the
Hyacinth is supposed to have originated in a
similar manner after Hyacinth had fallen a victim
to the jealousy of Zephyr. The **Aspasia** bears the
name of Aspasia of Miletus, the mistress of Pericles.
The term **Orchid** comes from the Greek *orchis,* a
testicle, all plants of this family being distinguished
by double testicles. The **Sweetbriar** is literally a
"fragrant thorn"; the **Lilac** betrays its Eastern
origin in the Turkish *leilak,* and Persian *lilaj ;* while
the term **Lavender** is derived from the Latin *lavere,*
to wash, because the essential oil obtained from this
shrub enters into the composition of a favourite
scent.

The **Dog-rose** was so called by the Greeks from
the belief that the root of this particular rose-tree
was efficacious in curing the bite of a mad dog.
The **Damask-rose** was brought to England from

Damascus by Dr. Linacre in 1540. The **Cabbage-rose** is thick and compact like a cabbage. The **Christmas-rose** makes its appearance about Christmas-time. The word **Primrose,** agreeably to the Latin *prima rosa,* signifies the first rose, or flower, of spring.

The **Mayflower,** otherwise the **Hawthorn,** the Anglo-Saxon for " hedge-thorn," appears in flower in the month of May, while **Gilly-flower** is merely a corruption of " July flower." The **Tiger-flower** is streaked like a tiger. **Daffodil** is a corruption of " d'Asphodele," the French name of this flower. **Hollyhock** is not " Holy Oak," but the Anglo-Saxon *holi-hoc,* or marsh mallow. The **Noontide,** or **Noon-flower,** closes its petals at noon ; the **Convolvulus,** so called from the Latin *con,* together, and *volvere,* to roll, does the like at sunset, in common with the ordinary field **Daisy,** which owes its name, a corruption of the Anglo-Saxon *doeges-eaye,* literally " the day's eye," to this circumstance. The **Butter-cup** was originally so designated in accordance with an old-established idea that the yellow hue of butter was attributable to the fact of these flowers being eaten by cattle. However, as the buttercups are invariably avoided by the cattle, the proverbial wisdom of our forefathers must for once in a way be discredited. **Cowslip** is a corruption of "cows' leek."

The very common supposition that the **Sunflower** inclines towards the sun is entirely erroneous, as has been proved by observation. This flower merely takes its name from its form and colour. On the other hand, if its etymology be correct, the **Heliotrope** does actually turn towards the sun, the word *helios* being Greek for sun, and *tropos*, to turn. The **Goldylocks** is so called on account of its tufts of yellow flowers; whereas the **Marigold,** which bears yellow flowers, was named in honour of Queen Mary. Both these, with the Sunflower, belong to the **Chrysanthemum** (Greek *chrusos*, gold, and *anthemos*, flower) family. The word **Rhododendron,** we may add, comes from the Greek *rhodon*, rose, and *dendron*, tree.

The **Passion-flower** symbolizes in its tints and several parts the various attributes of Christ's Passion, as follows:—The white tint, purity; the blue tint, heaven; the leaf, the spear; the five anthers, the five wounds; the tendrils, the whips and cords; the column of the ovary, the pillar of the cross; the stamens, the hammers; the three styles, the nails; the fleshy thorns within the flowers, the crown of thorns; the calyx, the nimbus, or glory. In addition to the foregoing the passion-flower remains open for three days, and this is supposed to correspond with the three years' ministry of the Redeemer.

Lastly, the flower known as the **Stock** received its name from the fact that it was principally sold in the old Stocks Market displaced by the building of the present Mansion House in the year 1737; the market itself having derived its title from a pair of stocks that stood there.

THE BIBLE.

IN the estimation of many millions of human beings the Bible is very properly regarded as the "Book of Books." And a Book of Books it truly is; not only THE Book above all others, but comprising a number of distinct works from the pens of various Inspired Writers according to the Old Law and the New. For this reason precisely the earliest Saxon version of the Sacred Volume was called the **Bible** in accordance with the Greek and Latin word *biblia*, the plural of *biblion*, a book, derived from *biblos*, the inner bark of the papyrus, which was the first kind of writing material known. "Bible," therefore, is a collective term for the **Scriptures**, which designation comes from the Latin *scriptura*, a writing, based upon the verb *scribere*, to write. Here, again, note the correct use of the plural.

The original translation of the Hebrew Testament into Greek, about the year 260 B.C., bore the title of the **Septuagint** because it employed the labours of seventy, or rather of seventy-two, translators. More than six hundred years afterwards, viz., in the Year of Our Lord 405, when St. Jerome (born 346, died 420) rendered the whole of the Scriptures—to be sure the New Testament had not an existence at the time of the Greek translation—into the Latin tongue, his performance was styled the *Vulgatus,* or **Vulgate,** from *vulgare,* to make known to the *vulgus,* the multitude. This **Latin Vulgate** constitues the Bible of the Roman Catholics as authorized by the Council of Trent in the year 1546. It was first printed for the use of the Christian world generally in 1462. The English translation of the Old Testament portion of the Vulgate bears the title of the **Douay Bible** because it was first printed and published at the English College at Douay, in France, in 1609. The New Testament portion, known as the **Rheims Bible,** was issued at Rheims twenty-seven years earlier, viz., in 1582.

The **Authorized Version** of the Bible appointed to be read in the Church of England is called **King James's Bible,** after James I., who ordered it to be prepared, and in whose reign (in the year 1611) it was first given to the people. The **Bishops' Bible,** published in parts between 1568 and 1572, derived its name from the seven bishops that assisted Archbishop Parker with his revision of **Cranmer's Bible,** otherwise **The Great Bible,** so called because Archbishop Cranmer's version of the text, published in 1539, was of large size, specially printed for the purpose of being displayed and read by the people in the churches. To the 1540 edition of this version Cranmer prefixed a lengthy Introduction. One of the earliest Latin Bibles, printed by Gutenberg between the years 1450 and 1455, and, indeed, one of the earliest perfect printed books from separate types, is known as the **Mazarin Bible,** from a copy being discovered in Cardinal Mazarin's library. The **Pearl Bible** was so called because it was printed in pearl type by Field in 1653. The **Geneva Bible,** printed at Geneva in 1560, also bears the singular title of the **Breeches Bible,** owing to the substitution of the word "breeches" for "aprons" in *Genesis* iii. 7. Similarly, the **Vinegar Bible** is indebted for its title to the misprinting of the word "vineyard" in the running headline to *Luke* xx. at the Clarendon Press in 1717; the **Beer Bible,** to the substitution of the words "the beer" for "strong drink" in the twenty-fourth chapter of *Isaiah,* ninth verse; the **Treacle Bible,** to the rendering of the passage, "Is there no balm in Gilead?" into "There is no more triacle at Gilaad" (*Jeremiah* viii. 22); the **Whig Bible,** to the misprinting of the word "peace-makers," so that the sentence reads, "Blessed are the placemakers"; the **Wicked Bible,** from the omission of a word in *Exodus* xx. 14, which caused the verse to read, "Thou shalt commit adultery"; and the **Bug Bible,** printed by John Daye in 1551, from the peculiar rendering of the fifth verse in *Psalm* xci., which reads, "So thou shalt not need to be afraid for any *bugs* by night, nor for the arrow that flieth by day." The first edition of the Authorized Version is called the **" He " Bible,** because it contains a misprint in *Ruth* iii. 15, the passage read-

ing, "And *he* went into the city." A subsequent
issue published in the same year, in which the
mistake is rectified, is known as the **" She " Bible.**
The **Virginia Bible** is a rare version of the Scriptures translated into the native language of the
North American Indians of Virginia. The first
edition of this Bible was printed in 1661–3, copies
of which are said to be worth £200.

The first five books of the Old Testament written
by Moses bear the collective title of the **Pentateuch**
on account of the two Greek words *penta,* five, and
teuchos, an implement, a tool, alluding to the Books
being the direct instrument of communication between God and His people. The titles of these five
Books themselves are as follows:—**Genesis,** which
expresses the Greek for origin or production, describes
the history of the world from its beginning; **Exodus,**
derived from *ex,* out, and *odus,* a way, narrates the
departure of the Israelites out of Egypt; **Leviticus**
sets forth the regulations affecting the priests and
Levites; **Numbers** contains the census of the
Israelites; and **Deuteronomy,** from the Greek
deuteros, second, and *nomos,* law, comprises the
second giving of the Law by Moses.

The designation **Apocrypha,** signifying hidden or
spurious, is applied to those Books whose authenticity
as Inspired Writings is not admitted; in other
words, to those portions of the Scriptures which,
inasmuch as they do not establish any doctrine, are
not held to be canonical, yet are such as, in the
words of the Prayer Book, "the Church doth read

for example of life and instruction of manners." On
the other hand, the **Apocalypse,** signifying disclo-
sure, is synonymous with the " Book of Revelation,"
and specifically applies to the concluding Book of
the Bible.

WINES.

WITH one or two exceptions only, the different kinds of wines owe their names to the places where they are produced. Thus, **Burgundy** and **Champagne** respectively come from the French provinces, **Pontac** from the town, and **Moselle** from the vineyards extensively cultivated on the banks of the river, so designated. Rhenish wines are popular all over Europe; yet none are probably more celebrated than the **Johannisberg**, produced at the Castle of Johannisberg (literally, John's Rock), near Wiesbaden, and **Hock**, produced at Hockheim. Among Italian wines, **Florence** comes from the historic "City of Flowers," whereas **Falernian**, celebrated by Martial, Horace, and other Latin authors, was made from grapes grown in the district around the ancient city of Falernum. A justly celebrated Tuscan wine is the **Montepulciano**, produced at the old city so denominated. As its name implies, **Malaga** is imported from Malaga, in Spain; **Sherry** is our English rendering of the place-name Xeres, near Cadiz; while **Port** constitutes the native wine of Oporto, the capital of Portugal. Of Mediterranean wines, **Cyprus**, brought from the now British island of

that name, and **Malmsey,** an English corruption of
Malvasia, so termed after the district in the island
of Candia, where it is produced, are the chief.
Madeira and **Canary** are imported from the islands
so called, situated on the great ocean highway to the
Cape of Good Hope.   An excellent wine greatly
sought after on the Continent, though somewhat
unknown in this country, is **Tokay,** produced from
white grapes cultivated in the district of Tokay,
Upper Hungary.   **Claret** owes its designation to
the French *clair*, clear, because it is a clarified wine;
whereas **Tent Wine** is a mere corruption of the
Spanish *vino tinto*, signifying a white wine coloured.
The sparkling champagne known as **Sillery** popu-
larizes the name of the Marquis de Sillery, the
proprietor of the vineyards where this particular
species is produced; just as **Pommery** is destined
to perpetuate the memory of Madame Pommery,
mother to the Duchess de Polignac, and sole
proprietress of the vineyards and subterranean
Pommery vaults near Rheims. **Moet and Chandon**
similarly denotes the champagne brewed by the
well-known French firm trading under the style of
" Moet et Chandon."

Among concoctions of the vinous order we have
Hippocras, so called because it is said to have
been first made according to the recipe of Hippo-
crates, the Father of Medicine ; **Badminton,**
originally prepared at Badminton, the seat of the
Duke of Beaufort; and **Negus,** named after Colonel
Francis Negus, who invented it.   Formerly, our

countrymen set great store by **Sack,** which was simply the designation of a dry wine, derived from the French word *sec*, dry.   Wine is said to be a **Dry Wine** when it is neither sweet nor sparkling.   It cannot be sweet because, the fermentation being complete, the sugar contained in it is fully decomposed ; moreover, it is dry because the carbonic acid has escaped.   For the like reason, a certain evidence that port wine has completed the process of fermentation is the collection of tartar in the interior of the bottle, forming a crust ; hence the term **Crusted Port.**   A very bad wine of whatever kind usually bears the name of **Three Men Wine,** owing to the idea that it requires one man to hold the drinker, and another to pour it down his throat, while the third is the unfortunate individual himself.   The derivation of the term **Wine** is the Anglo-Saxon *vin* from the Latin *vinum*, allied to *vinea*, a vine.

LITERARY SOBRIQUETS.

GILDAS, the earliest chronicler of British history (born 511, died 570), was surnamed **The Wise** on account of his learning, which must have excited the wonder of the semi-barbarian inhabitants of these islands in the sixth century. Later, the Saxon historian Beda, incorrectly called Bede (born 673, died 735), was surnamed **The Venerable** because he was also an ecclesiastic. Approaching more modern times, we meet with John White, a Nonconformist lawyer, who, in consequence of being the author of a work entitled "The First Century of Scandalous, Malignant Priests, made and admitted into Benefices by the Prelates, &c.," merited the popular description of **Century White.** Still nearer our own day, Matthew Gregory Lewis (born 1775, died 1818) became the recipient of the name of **Monk Lewis,** after the publication of his famous novel, "The Monk"; just as John Thomas Smith, the antiquary (born 1766, died 1833), was indebted to his chatty, albeit valuable work, "A Book for a Rainy Day," for his sobriquet of **Rainy-Day Smith.**

Turning to the poets, John Sylvester, the translator of Du Barta's "Divine Weeks and Works" (born 1563, died 1613), is popularly referred to as **Silver-tongued Sylvester** on account of the sweet melody of his verse. John Taylor, the **Water Poet** (born 1580, died 1654), was a Thames waterman; James Hogg, **The Ettrick Shepherd** (born 1772, died 1835), followed the employment of a shepherd in the forest of Ettrick, Selkirkshire; and Edward Capern, **The Bidëford Postman** (born 1819), was for several years a letter-carrier in the little town of Bidëford, Devonshire. Nathaniel Lee (born 1655, died 1691) received the name of **The Mad Poet** from the fact of his four years' confinement in a mad-house. **The Quaker Poet** was Bernard Barton, the friend of Charles Lamb (born 1784, died 1849); while Samuel Rogers, **The Banker Poet** (born 1763, died 1855), divided his time pleasantly between the counting-house and the study. Thomas Moore (born 1779, died 1852) merited the style of **Anacreon Moore** by his translations from the Greek poet Anacreon, and the circumstance that his own original verses were constructed upon the same classic model. Richard Horne, the poet and critic (born 1802, died 1884), was known as **Orion Horne,** and also as **The Farthing Poet,** on account of his principal work "Orion," published at one farthing, as a satire on the poverty of the book-buying public.

Sir Walter Scott (born 1771, died 1832) was surnamed **The Wizard of the North** owing to the magic influence which he exerted over all classes of the people, and the widespread fascination of his novels; while Henry Mackenzie, the author of "The Man of Feeling" (born 1745, died 1831), enjoyed the signal honour of being designated **The Addison of the North,** owing to the purity and excellence of his style. No more flattering recognition of the genius of William Wordsworth (born 1770, died 1850) could ever have been desired than the title of **The Minstrel of the Border,** bestowed upon him by Sir Walter Scott. **The Corn Law Rhymer** was Ebenezer Elliott (born 1781, died 1849) who, by the dedication of his numerous versified philippics to the opponents of Free Trade, indirectly, if not directly, prepared the way for the repeal of the obnoxious Corn Laws in the year 1846. Reference to the word " Philippics " carries us back in imagination to Demosthenes, who directed one of his most famous orations against Philip, King of Macedon; hence, any indignant invective or vehement denunciation is characteristically styled a PHILIPPIC.

THE COUNTIES OF ENGLAND AND WALES.

NORTHUMBERLAND originally denoted the land north of the Humber; **Cumberland,** the land occupied by the Cymri; and **Westmoreland,** the land of the Westmorings, or people of the Western moors. **Durham** is a corruption of *Dunholm,* signifying a hill-fort on an island in the river; *dun* being Celtic for a hill, or fort on a hill, and *holm* the Scandinavian for an island. The Shire, or County, of **York,** in common with the majority of the Midland and Welsh counties, is named after its chief town; or rather, in this case, the ancient city described in documents as *Eurewic,* but pronounced *Yorric,* from its position on the river Eure, now known as the Ouse.

Lancashire indicates the Shire of **Lancaster,** the *caester,* or camp-town, on the Lune. This Anglo-Saxon word *Caester,* derived from the Latin *castra,* a camp, fortress, appears also in the names of **Cheshire,** a contraction of *Caestershire,* the Shire of **Chester,** the town built on the site of the old Roman *castra,* or camp; in **Leicestershire,** the Shire of the camp-town on the river *Leire,* now called the Soar; in **Worcestershire,** the Shire of

Hwic-ware-shire, or fortress-town, of the Huiccii;
and in **Gloucestershire,** the Shire of the camp-
town in which *Gloi,* a son of the Emperor Claudius,
was born during the Roman occupation of Britain.

Lincoln is a contraction of the Latin *Lindum-
colonia,* signifying the colony formed by the Romans
on the *Llyn-dun,* literally "the fortified hill by the
pool," originally occupied and so called by the
ancient Britons [*see* LONDON]. The names **Norfolk**
and **Suffolk** respectively indicate those portions of
the eastern coast settled by the Angles, who separated into two distinct tribes, viz., the north folk and
the south folk. **Essex** is a contraction of *East-
seaxe,* denoting the territory occupied by the East
Saxons; **Sussex,** of *Suth-seaxe,* or South Saxons;
and **Middlesex,** of *Middle-seaxe,* or the inhabitants
of the district between Essex and **Wessex,** the
land of the West Saxons, which, under the Hep-
tarchy, extended to the westward as far as
Devon. **Surrey** is a modification of the Anglo-
Saxon *Suth-rey,* south of the river, *i.e.,* the
Thames. **Kent** was formerly *Cantium,* indicating
the land bestowed upon Canute, one of the companions of Brute, an early King of Britain, who,
according to Geoffrey of Monmouth, settled in
England and eventually founded the Danish
dynasty.

Hampshire, also written **Hants,** expresses the
Shire of *Hantone,* or *Hantune,* now known as
Southampton, the south town on the river Ant,
or Southampton Water. **Dorset** was originally

Dwrset, a compound of the Celtic *dwr,* water, and the Anglo-Saxon *set,* a settlement, alluding to the early settlement of this district by a tribe of Britons who styled themselves *Dwr-trigs,* or "water-dwellers." **Somerset** is a corruption of the Anglo-Saxon *Suth-morset,* literally "the south-moor-settlement." **Devon** is a modified form of *Dwfuient,* the Celtic for "the deep valleys." An earlier name for this portion of Britain was *Damnonia,* the territory of the Damnonii, a Celtic tribe. **Cornwall** denotes the territory of the "foreigners in the horn," agreeably to the Latin *cornu,* a horn, referring to its numerous promontories, and its inhabitants the *Wahl,* the Saxon term for "foreigners." Like Wales, this portion of our island was never invaded by the Anglo-Saxons; consequently its people, the Cymri, a branch of the Celts, were left in undisturbed possession [*see* WALES]. The Duchy of Cornwall is still included in the Principality of Wales. **Wiltshire** only partly expresses the Shire of **Wilton**, a contraction of *Willy-town,* or the town on the river Willy. **Berkshire** is a modern spelling of the Anglo-Saxon *Bearoc-scire,* "forest shire," in allusion to the forest districts of Bagshot and Windsor; while **Buckingham** was originally described as *Boccenham,* the Anglo-Saxon for "beech-tree-home," this county being especially noted for its beeches.

Oxford derived its name from the *Ox-ford* over the Isis; **Hertford,** from the ford crossed by harts; **Hereford,** from the army ford; and **Stafford,** from the ford crossed by means of staves or stilts.

Bedford is a contraction of *Bedican ford*, the Anglo-Saxon for "the protected ford." **Cambridge** owes its name to the University town by the bridge over the *Cam*, or crooked river [*see* CAMBERWELL]. **Huntingdon** was anciently a great deer forest, and therefore much resorted to for hunting. **North-ampton** is a corruption of *North-avon-town*, alluding to its position north of the river *Neu*, in olden times known as the Avon. **Rutland** expresses the Anglo-Saxon for "red land," referring to the colour of its soil. **Warwick** is the modern description of the Anglo-Saxon *Waer-wic*, signifying the garrison, or war town. **Nottingham** is a corruption of *Snot-ingaham*, "the place of caves," so called on account of the soft sandstone which so greatly facilitated the formation of caverns during the early history of our country; as *e.g.*, "Mortimer's hole," and the subterranean passage that led thereto from Nottingham Castle in the reign of Edward III. **Derby** is a contraction of the Saxon *Deer-by*, or "wild-beast village," doubtless so designated from its frequent invasion by strange animals from the mountainous district of "The Peak" in search of prey. **Shrop-shire** denotes the Shire of *Scrobbesburgh*, the Anglo-Saxon for "shrub-town," modified by the Normans into *Sloppesburie* (from which the present town of **Salop** derived its name), and corrupted in modern times into **Shrewsbury**. **Monmouth** indicates the county that includes the mouth of the *Mon*, originally described as the *Mynwy*, "the border river."

Anglesea, properly *Anglesey* [*see* CHELSEA, &c.], is one of the three counties of Wales whose names are not essentially Welsh. Thus, **Glamorgan** signifies the *Gwlad-Morgan*, or territory of Morgan, a chieftain who lived in the tenth century; **Brecknock** is the hill of Brecon, or Brychan, a Welsh prince; **Radnor** is a modern spelling of *Rhiadnwr-Gwy*, meaning " the Cataract of the Wye"; **Montgomery** refers to the fortress built on the *mont*, or height, by Roger de Montgomerie, in 1093; **Denbigh** was originally *Dinbach*, the Celtic and Cymric for " a little fort"; **Flint** was so called from the quantity of quartz found in this county; **Carnarvon** owes its origin to *Cær-yu-ar-Fon*, the *cær*, or fortress, on the *arfon*, or water; **Carmarthen** denotes the fortress erected by Merlin; **Merioneth** was named after Merion, an early British saint; **Cardigan** indicates the territory of Ceredig, a Welsh chieftain; while **Pembroke** signifies the *pen*, or head of the *broc*, the Celtic and Cymric for a district, so called because this promontory was virtually the Land's End.

CARRIAGES.

THE **Phaeton** owes its designation to the mythological personage of that name who received permission to drive the sun-car of Helios, his father, for one day, with the result that, being overthrown, he nearly set the world on fire. The **Victoria** was introduced in the year that witnessed the coronation of Her Majesty Queen Victoria. The **Clarence** was the favourite conveyance of the Duke of Clarence, afterwards William IV. The **Brougham,** invented in 1839, received its name from Lord Brougham, who was the first to permanently adopt it; and the same may be said of the **Stanhope,** so called in compliment to Lord Stanhope. The **Sociable** is an appropriate name enough for an open carriage of which the facing seats afford opportunity for pleasant conversation. The **Landau** was first made at Landau in Germany; whereas the **Tilbury** perpetuates the name of a celebrated London sportsman who introduced this particular species of carriage during the early part of the present century.

The small, light, one-horse vehicle known as a **Dog-cart** is so called because such a one was originally constructed for sportsmen to drive their pointers and setters (which they kept in a box under the seat) to the scene of the sport. The term **Buggy** is a corruption of *Bourgeois*, a French name indicating a vehicle intended for the middle classes so denominated; while **Gig** is a contraction of the Italian *giga*, a romp, and the French *gigue*, a lively dance, a jig, in allusion to its jumping and rocking motion. The like derivation applies to the long, light ship's wherry which passes under the same name. The term **Sulky,** as applied to a light two-wheeled conveyance, owed its origin to the fact that, when it was introduced, people hazarded the opinion that none but sulky, morose, and selfish people would ride in such a carriage, because it had only accommodation for one person. The **Noddy,** peculiar to Dublin, derives its title from the jolting motion which keeps its riders continually nodding; and the **Jaunting Car,** from the jaunts and country outings for which, on the other side of the Irish Sea, these vehicles are largely employed. The English **Break** bears its name because it partakes of the character of the four-wheel vehicle used by horse-breakers; indeed, it differs from the latter only in the addition of the upper portion containing the seats.

Stage-coaches were originally so called on account of the different stages at which they stopped to change horses and refresh the passengers. **'Bus** is short for **Omnibus,** a Latin word signifying "for all." The step at the back of an omnibus is facetiously styled the **Monkey-board,** in consequence of the capers usually executed thereon by the conductor. The board on either side of the roof of the vehicle, upon which theatrical and other advertisements are exhibited is known as the **Knife-board,** from its fancied resemblance to that article of domestic utility. So far from having derived its name from one of the northern suburbs of London, a **Hackney-coach** is simply an English rendering of *coche-a-haquence*, the literal French for a coach drawn by a hired horse. The word **Coach** (French, *coche*, the diminutive of the Italian *conchula*, a shell) really means a shell-like contrivance upon wheels. **Cab** is a contraction of the **Cabriolet,** from *cabriole*, a goat's leap, in allusion to its lightness and springiness, first introduced in Paris. This vehicle, after undergoing sundry changes and improvements, was patented in the year 1883 as the "Safety Cab" by Joseph Aloysius Hansom, from which circumstance it has in more recent times come to be generally designated the **Hansom Cab.**

The term **Hearse** traces its origin through the German *hirsch* from the Gothic *hersa*, a sepulchral mound. At a later date it implied a temporary monument, but nowadays it denotes the funeral car. The word **Funeral,** by the way, is a contraction of the Latin *funeralis*, signifying a torchlight procession, from *funis*, a torch, because interments among the Romans always took place by night. **Pantech-nicon** is a Greek word, composed of *pan*, all, and *techne*, art, indicative of the place where every kind of industrial art was exhibited or exposed for sale In modern days the term has come to be exclusively applied to a vehicle constructed for the removal of household furniture. Lastly, the cloth that covers the box-seat of a carriage of any kind is called the **Hammer-cloth,** because in the old coaching days it concealed the box which contained a hammer, nails, and other implements useful for repairs in the event of a breakdown on the journey.

DANCES.

ANCING is styled the **Terpsichorean Art** in honour of Terpsichore, the daughter of Jupiter and Mnemosyne, whom the ancients regarded as its inventress. The **Morris Dance,** from which our "Jack in the Green" and his fellow May-day revellers trace their origin, was the military dance of the Moors, or Moriscoes, introduced into this country by John of Gaunt on his return from Spain in the reign of Edward III. Five men and a boy took part in it, and from the fact of the boy wearing an ill-fitting helmet called a *morione*, he received the name of "Mad Morion," which was subsequently corrupted into **Maid Marian.** The **Saraband** was invented by Zarabanda, a famous dancer of Seville in the sixteenth century. The **Gavotte** arose among the Gavots, a people who inhabited the department of the Upper Alps and the province of Dauphiny, in France. **Quadrille** is the literal French for "a little square," so called from the position taken up by the dancers; while the **Lancers** derived their name from a company of Lancers who originally improvised this variation of the Quadrille for their own amusement while seated in their saddles. The **Polka,** of Polish origin, is so designated on account of the Bohemian word *pulka*, a half, in allusion to the half step occurring in it; the **Schottische** is a variation of the 'Polka; the **Mazourka** is the national dance of Poland—all of which, with the addition of the **Redowa,** are native terms. The **Waltz** is a contraction of the German **Waltzer,** derived from the verb *waltzen*, to roll, to revolve, alluding to the revolutions made by the pairs of dancers placed *vis-à-vis*. The **Country Dance,** so far from being a peasants' dance, is nothing more than a corruption of the French *contre-danse*, signifying that the parties place themselves opposite to each other during the dance. Strictly speaking, the Contre-danse and the Quadrille are one and the same. The **Roger de Coverley** derived its name from the great-grand-father of Roger de Coverley, or rather, to be precise, of Roger of Cowley, near Oxford, who invented it. The **Minuet** (Latin *minutus*, small) is so called wholly on account of the short steps peculiar to this dance. The **Tarantella** was invented in Italy out of the supposition that the profuse perspiration which it induced was a certain cure for the poisonous bite of the TARANTULA SPIDER, named after the city of Taranto, where its baneful presence was first manifested. **Cinderella Dances** are those which terminate before midnight, in allusion to Cinderella of nursery renown.

The origin of the word **Ball,** in its application to a dancing-party, is somewhat singular. Centuries ago there was in vogue on the Continent a three.

fold game, in which the players danced to the sound
of their own voices while they threw to one another
a ball. In all probability this arose out of the
curious " Ball-Play in Church " by the Neapolitans
during the Saturnalia, or " Feast of Fools," corresponding to our Easter-tide. There is even now a
statute in existence which regulated the size and
character of the ball to be used on such occasions.
In opening the ceremony, the Dean took the ball in
his left hand, and commenced an antiphon, which
the organ took up; whereupon he tossed the ball to
first one and then another of the choir-boys, as they
joined hands, sang, and danced around him. When,
therefore, the three-fold game alluded to above
divided and its three sets of dancers became
independent of each other, the dance itself took
the name of the article that was, as if by common
consent, discarded—to wit, *the ball;* and the song
was styled the *Ballata,* or, according to the modern
English, a BALLAD indicative of a dancing-song;
while the verb *ballare,* to dance, gave existence to
the French **Ballet,** signifying a dance tune. *Apropos*
of the Ballet, the term **Coryphee,** as applied to a
ballet-dancer, traces its origin from the Greek
coryphœus, the designation of one who danced to
the lute in the theatres of the ancients. *En passant,*
the famous war dance of the Greeks, executed in
very quick time and known as the **Phyrric Dance,**
was so denominated after Pyrrichos, a celebrated
Dorian flautist.

The **Hornpipe** is an inversion of *pib-gorn,* the

name of the old Welsh instrument consisting of a *pib*, or pipe, with a *gorn*, or horn, at each end, to which this dance was originally stepped ; the **Reel** has reference to the whirling evolutions performed by the dancer, as of winding cotton on a reel ; whereas the **Jig** comes from the French *gigue*, a lively dance, and *gige*, a stringed instrument, the usual accompaniment to this rough-and-ready style of pedal exhilaration. The term **Breakdown** is an Americanism, denoting the last boisterous dance before the breaking *up* of a dancing-party towards early morning. Appropriately enough, such a dance invariably constitutes the final item of a negro-minstrel entertainment.

PIGMENTS AND DYES.

THE word **Pigment** is a contraction of the Latin *pigmentum*, based upon the verb *pingere*, to paint. **Dye** traces its origin to the Anglo-Saxon *deag*, a colour, remotely derived from the Latin *tingere*, to stain. Several of the pigments most generally used owe their names to the places whence they are, or were originally, brought. As examples: **Umber** was first obtained in the district of **Umbria,** in Italy, and **Sienna,** properly called *Terra di Sienna*, or Sienna Earth, from Sienna; **Gamboge** comes from Cambodia, formerly known as Gambogia, in Siam; **Indigo,** from Indicus, the ancient description of India; and **Krems White,** from the city of Krems, in Austria, where it is exclusively manufactured. **Prussian Red, Brunswick Green, Brunswick Black, Frankfort Black, Hamburg Lake, Venetian Red,** and **Chinese Yellow,** speak for themselves. **Prussian Blue,** also called **Berlin Blue,** was first made by a native colourman of Berlin in the year 1710; whereas **Saunders Blue** is merely a corruption of *cendres-bleus*, the French for blue ashes, this pigment being obtained from calcined bluestone. Another name for the latter is **Ultramarine,** because it was originally brought from *ultra*, beyond, and *marinus*, the sea.

The deep blue known as **Mazarine** was named after Cardinal Mazarin, the Prime Minister of France (born 1602, died 1661), in whose time it was first prepared; while the puce colour known as **Pompadour** received its designation from Madame le Pompadour, the mistress of Louis XV. (born 1721, died 1764), who popularized it. **Cardinal** is so called because it expresses the exact shade of the red habit worn by the cardinals of the Church ; the term **Carmine** owes its origin to the Italian *carminio*, purple ; while **Carnation** denotes a flesh tint, in accordance with the Latin *caro*, flesh. The colour which results from the combination of a vivid red with more or less white is styled **Pink,** owing to its resemblance to the flower so designated.

The origin of the word **Purple** must be sought in connection with the circumstance in which this dye, or colour, was discovered. It appears that one day a favourite dog belonging to Hercules of Tyre chanced to eat a species of fish known to the ancients as the *purpura* ; and upon returning to his master, the latter found the lips of the animal tinged with the colour that was shortly afterwards imitated and denominated *purple*. The term **Scarlet** is a modification of *sakarlat*, the Persian description of a bright red colour; while **Crimson** traces its existence through the Old English *crimosyn* to *garmaz*, the Arabic term for the cochineal insect, from whose dried body, found upon a species of cactus, this vivid

dye-stuff is obtained.   The beautiful purple obtained
from chloride of gold bears the name of **Cassius**
after its inventor.

Magenta was named in commemoration of the
Battle of Magenta, fought in 1859; and **Vandyke
Brown,** from its having been so frequently used by
Vandyk (born 1599, died 1641) that it forms a
characteristic colour in all his portraits. **Sepia** is
the Greek designation of the cuttle-fish, and the
pigment so called is obtained from the dark juice
secreted by the glands of the Indian species of this
fish. **Sap-Green** is prepared from the juice of the
ripe berries of the buckthorn; whereas **Emerald
Green** denotes the particular shade of green that
characterizes the emerald.   **Lamp Black** is so
called because it was originally obtained from the
burning of resinous matter over a lamp. **Ivory
Black** is a pigment formerly obtained from charred
ivory, but nowadays from bones.   The origin of
Isabel, a dull brownish-yellow, with a mixture of
red and grey, is as follows :—When the Duke of
Austria was besieging Ostend in 1601, Isabella, his
wife, the daughter of Philip II. of Spain, vowed that
she would not change her linen until the town had
been taken.   Unfortunately for her personal comfort,
the town held out for two years, at the end of which
period her linen assumed the characteristic hue that
was afterwards imitated by the ingenious colourman who sought to honour her by perpetuating the
incident.

LONDON DISTRICTS AND SUBURBS.

A T that remote period when the first rude huts were established on the banks of the Thames, the surrounding scene could have presented nothing more inviting to the eye than an extensive marsh or morass. That such was undoubtedly the case the existing names of FENCHURCH Street and FINSBURY, furnish ample evidence. The former marks the site of an ancient church situated among the fens, while the latter is an easy corruption of *Fensbury*, the Anglo-Saxon designation for " a town among the fens." Therefore it was not surprising that the barbaric Britons, who founded what we now call **London,** should have given the name of *Llyn-dun* [*see* LINCOLN] to their colony beside the Thames. *Apropos* of the **Thames,** the name of our noble river is merely a slight contraction of the Latin *Thamesis*, signifying " the broad Isis." **Isis** is the Celtic for water.

Westminster was denominated after the Abbey [*see* WESTMINSTER ABBEY]. **Belgravia** is the name given to the fashionable district of which Belgrave Square is the common centre. **Pimlico** owed its designation to an attempt on the part of the tavern-

keepers of this neighbourhood to rival the celebrated
nut-brown ales of one Ben Pimlico, who kept a
pleasure-garden near Hoxton, the road to which
was known as **Pimlico Walk** (still in existence),
and the garden itself, first as " Pimlico's," and subsequently as " Pimlico." The name of **Knightsbridge** carries us back to the time when two knights,
on their way to receive a blessing from the Bishop
of London at Fulham, engaged in a deadly combat
on the bridge that spanned the Westbourne, exactly
on the spot where Albert Gate now stands. Prior
to this incident the bridge had borne the name of
Fulham Bridge. **Mayfair** occupies the site of an
annual six days' fair held in May, originally at the
instance of Edward I., for the benefit of the leper
hospital of St. James the Less, Bishop of Jerusalem,
now St. James's Palace. The district of **Soho** was
known by its present name as long ago as the sixteenth century ; " *So ho !* " being the cry of the
huntsmen when calling off their harriers in the days
when the whole of London west of Drury Lane
was open country. **Bloomsbury** is a corruption of
" Lomesbury Village," of which the Manor House
stood on the site of Bloomsbury Square. **Smithfield** is a modern perversion of " Smoothfield," an
extensive tract of meadow land where horses were
sold and tournaments were held as far back as the
twelfth century. The first recorded English horse-
race was witnessed in Smoothfield in the year 1154.
Clerkenwell derived its name from an ancient well
(now marked by an iron pump let into the wall at

the south-east end of Ray Street) beside which the parish clerks performed their Miracle Plays. **Spa Fields,** now built over, owed their designation to a medicinal well, or Spa, discovered in 1206, and subsequently known as " The London Spa." The proper description of **Bunhill Fields** is *Bonhill, i.e.,* " good hill " Fields, so styled because the victims of the Great Plague were buried here in 1665. **Moorfields** was formerly a bleak moor skirting the northern portion of the marshy land known as Fensbury, now **Finsbury,** already referred to.

Shoreditch did not receive its name from Jane Shore, neither is the word a corruption of " Sewer Ditch," as some writers have suggested. This district really comprised the manor of Sir John Soerditch, a wealthy London citizen and a valiant knight who fought by the side of Edward the Black Prince at Crecy and Poictiers. **Whitechapel** was designated after the White Chapel of St. Mary, built in 1673. **Goodman's Fields** perpetuated the name of the owner of the land now known as the Minories, upon which a Priory of the Nuns of St. Clare was afterwards built. **Shadwell** is a corruption of St. Chad's Well, discovered in this neighbourhood in ancient times. The once-notorious **Ratcliffe Highway** derived its name from the Manor of Ratcliffe, belonging to the adjoining parish of Stepney. The title has now been changed to St. George's Street. **Stepney** was anciently described as *Stebenhithe,* signifying that it contained a wharf or haven belonging to one Steben or Steven. **Spitalfields** marks

the site of the ancient Priory of St. Mary of the
Spittle, dissolved in 1534. The French refugees
established the silk manufacture here in 1685.
Bethnal Green recalls the existence of the old
family of the Bathons, whose history is first recorded
in connection with their property situated in this
neighbourhood during the reign of Edward I.
Hoxton is a corruption of *Hogsdon,* meaning hog's
town. In proof of this statement we may add that
Hog Lane still exists in the vicinity. **De Beauvoir
Town** preserves the family name of the De Beau-
voirs, whose original ancestor, Richard de Beauvoir,
of Guernsey, resided here in princely style. **Copen-
hagen Fields** were so called after a tea-house
opened by a Dane, about the time when the King of
Denmark paid a visit to James I. **Haggerstone** is
a corruption of " Hergotestan," the literal Saxon
for " Our God's Town." **Hackney** was originally
described as *Hackoneye,* signifying an *ey,* or portion
of well-watered pasture land, appropriated by a
Danish chief named Hacon [*see* Chelsea, &c.].

Dalston is properly *Daleston,* or Vale-town.
This was a quiet suburban village situated in a
valley during the days when the northern districts
of the Metropolis were more or less wooded—as
witness **Stoke Newington,** or the new town in the
meadow by the wood. The word *Stoke* comes from
the Anglo-Saxon *stoc,* a wood or stockade ; *ton* is the
Old English for town, and *ing* the Anglo-Saxon
for a meadow, also a family settlement. **Southgate**
is expressive of the southern entrance to the en-

closure, anciently known as Enfield Chase; and
Kingsland the royal domain adjacent to it.
Abney Park owes its name to ABNEY HOUSE,
recently converted into a Conservative Club, but
originally the residence of Sir Thomas Abney
(born 1639, died 1722), Lord Mayor and a distinguished Nonconformist, knighted by William III.
Dr. Isaac Watts died at Abney House in 1748.
Green Lanes indicates the rural character of this
neighbourhood in bygone times. **Edmonton** is
properly *Edmond's-town.* The name of **Ball's Pond**
is all that remains to remind us of the one-time
existence of "The Salutation" house of call which
had a pond for dog and duck sports, kept by John
Ball. **Mildmay Park** is so called after MILDMAY
HOUSE, the family seat of Sir Henry Mildmay, who
came into possession of the estate by his marriage
with the daughter of William Halliday, an Alderman
of the City in the time of Charles I. **Muswell
Hill** is a slight corruption of *Mustwell Hill,* derived
from the Latin *mustus,* new, fresh; because on
this hill there was anciently discovered a well of
clear, fresh water by the friars of St. John's Priory,
Clerkenwell, who had a dairy hereabouts. That
portion of the hill which has been cut through for the
construction of the line of railway to Enfield, Barnet,
and the north, bears the name of **The Hog's Back,**
in allusion to its shape. The name of **Wood Green**
is self-explanatory. **Hornsey** is a corruption of
"Harringe," or meadow of hares. **Canonbury**
received its title from the residence of the Prior of

the Canons of St. Bartholomew, built in this neighbourhood soon after the Conquest. *Bury* is Saxon
for a town or enclosed habitation, equivalent to the
Celtic *don*, and Old English *ton*. In days of old,
Highbury contained a Priory of the Knights of St.
John of Jerusalem, built in 1271. The establishment
was called *High-bury*, because it stood upon higher
ground than their previous residence which had borne
the name of *Tolentone*, or lower town. **Holloway**
reminds us that this was once a miry hollow between
Highgate and Islington. **Barnsbury** is a corruption
of *Berners-bury*, originally a manor belonging to Lady
Juliana Berners, Abbess of St. Albans. **Islington**
has always been a favourite suburb in modern
times, and even our mediæval ancestors must have
been delighted with its situation, lying high and
dry beyond the fens and the sloughy neighbourhood
of the " old bourne." Its name signifies "the
settlement of the Islings."

King's Cross derived its name from a wretched
statue of George IV., set up in honour of his
accession in 1820, and demolished to make way for
the London terminus of the Great Northern Railway in 1842. The parish of **St. Pancras** is so
called after the church dedicated to the boy-saint
who was martyred by Diocletian in the early days
of Christianity. **Agar Town,** now entirely swept
away by modern improvements, was designated after
William Agar, a miserly lawyer who acquired the
lease of the land for building purposes in 1840.
Somers Town is the property of Lord Somers, and

Camden Town, of the Earl of Camden. **Kentish Town** was formerly written " Kestestown " ; but even that was a corruption of " Kantelowes Town," erected upon the Manor of Kantelowes. The modern spelling of this family name is *Cantlowes*. **Primrose Hill** is still a pleasant eminence whereon primroses grow, despite the encroachments of bricks and mortar all around. **Highgate** is a title expressive of the elevated situation of the village that sprang up around the toll-gate established on the common highway from Barnet to Gray's Inn Road about the year 1400. **Holly Village,** Highgate, was so called by its foundress, the Baroness Burdett-Coutts-Bartlett, after her residence, Holly Lodge, hard by. **Hampstead** signifies a farmhouse or homestead. The word is Saxon : *ham*, a home, and *stede*, a place. In its wider sense, *ham* denotes a town. The western slope of Hampstead bears the name of **Frognal,** after Frognal Priory, an ambitious edifice built here by Memory-Corner Thompson (born 1757, died 1843), in imitation of Horace Walpole's toy village on Strawberry Hill. **Bishop's Wood,** Hampstead, comprised the private estate of the Bishop of London, at the time when that ecclesiastic resided at Highgate. **Gospel Oak** received its designation from the oak that marked the boundaries of Hampstead and St. Pancras, and under which, in accordance with an ancient custom, the Gospel was read once a year. John Whitfield is said to have preached under this oak. **Chalk Farm** is a corruption of " Chalcot Farm," a picturesque farmhouse in whose vicinity duels were usually fought during the century gone by. **St. John's Wood** was anciently a thickly wooded district sheltering an "Abbey of the Holy Virgins of St. John the Baptist." **Kilburn** owes its name to the *Kil*, the Celtic word for a cell, occupied by "one Godwyne, a holy hermit," beside the *bourne*, or brook. **Maida Vale** was so called in commemoration of the Battle of Maida, in which the English defeated the French, July 4, 1806. **Marylebone** does not signify "Mary the Good," as the majority of Londoners imagine, but "St. Mary of the Bourne," alluding to the church of St. Mary within sight of the bourne that ran from the hermit's cell at *Kilbourne* down to **Tyburn,** or rather *Twa-burne;* so called because two different bournes, or streams, met in the neighbourhood where the Marble Arch now stands.

The name of **Bayswater** has undergone considerable change from the original. Not so very long ago the whole of this district was known as **Bayswater Fields;** during the last century it bore the name of "Bear's Watering," and previously that of *Baynard's Watering.* By the last was meant the land dotted with pools held from the Manor of Westminster, by Ralph Baynard, the favourite of William the Conqueror, who resided at BAYNARD'S CASTLE, at Blackfriars, on the north bank of the Thames. These pools, together with the Tyburn were converted into what is now styled the SERPENTINE, owing to its form, in 1733. **Paddington,** originally written *Padynton,* was the settlement or town of the Pædings, a branch of the family who originally established themselves at, and gave their name to, *Padendene,* in Surrey. **Westbourne Park** derived its name from the west bourne, or stream, that wended its way from the hermit's cell at "Kilbourne," in the direction of the "Baynard's Watering," and thence, after passing under Fulham (or Knights') Bridge, emptied itself into the Thames. **Notting Hill** is a corruption of *Knolton Barn* (*Hill*), a manor held by the De Veres, and subsequently by Robert Fenroper, an Alderman of the City, in the reign of Henry VIII. The name of **Shepherd's Bush** once more puts us in mind of the pastoral character of the environs of London in the days gone by. **Acton** is an Anglo-Saxon name for "Oak town," signifying the town built in the vicinity of the large Oak Forest. **Gunnersbury** denotes the town, or enclosed habitation, named after Gunylda, the niece of King Canute, who resided here during the Danish occupation of England. **Kew** was anciently described in documents as *Kay-hoo,* meaning a quay situated on a *hoo,* or *hoe,* the Scandinavian for a spit of land. **Brentford** signifies the ford over the Brent, a tributary of the Thames that takes its rise near Hendon. **Isleworth** means a manor beside the water. The first portion of the word comes from the Celtic, *Isis,* water; the second is Anglo-Saxon for a manor. **Staines** owes its name to the boundary stone (Saxon *stane,* a stone) by the river, which displays the words "God preserve the City of London."

The date of this stone is 1280. **Kingston** was designated after the King's stone, now preserved within railings near the Town Hall, upon which the Saxon monarchs sat to be anointed. **Shepperton** is Old English for *Shepherd's Town*, or the abode of shepherds. The name of **Twickenham** denotes a hamlet situated between two tributaries of the Thames. **Richmond** was anciently known as **Sheen**, a Saxon term for "resplendent," in allusion to the palace erected by Edward I. When Henry VII. rebuilt the palace, after its destruction by fire in 1479, he changed the name of the village to Richmond, in perpetuation of his title of Earl of Richmond prior to ascending the throne. This king died here in 1509.

Chiswick is a corruption of "Cheoselwick," derived from the Anglo-Saxon *ceosel*, sand, gravel, and the Teutonic *wick*, a reach, from the root *waes*, a moist meadow. **Hammersmith** was originally *Hammersmeide*, a Saxon village distinguished for the number of its smithies. The forename, *Hammer*, is Scandinavian for a village or small town. **Kensington** derived its name, or rather that of *Kynsington*, the Saxon for King's meadow, with the Old English suffix *ton*, a town, from a royal residence erected here in very early times. **Brompton** was so called from the broom-trees that grew in the neighbourhood of this healthy *ton* or town. **Chelsea** is described in old documents as "Chevelsey,' meaning shingle island. The first portion of the word claims the same etymology as Chiswick, viz., *ceosel*, sand, gravel; while the suffix *ey*, or *ea*, is also Anglo-Saxon, derived from *oe*, the Scandinavian for running water. These terminals always indicate water, and not unfrequently an island, properly so called; as, for example, Anglesey, the Isle of the Angles. In the case of Hackney the terminal is expressive of a well-watered pasture, as has already been seen; whereas in the cases of Chelsea and Battersea the allusion is not merely to their proximity to the Thames, but to their partial isolation in ancient times from the adjacent land on account of the creeks and inlets of the river. **Battersea,** we may here remark, is described in Domesday Book as "the Manor of Patricesy"; but even this early name was a corruption of Petersey, or St. Peter's-ey, because it had belonged to the Abbey of St. Peter's, Westminster, from time out of mind. To return: **Walham Green** denotes a settlement of foreigners; *wal*, being a modification of *wahl*, the Celtic for foreign, and *ham*, the Old English for a home. **Fulham** was formerly written "Fullenhame," the Anglo-Saxon for a habitation of waterfowl. **Parson's Green** received its name from the parsonage in connection with Fulham Church that stood here previous to 1740. **Percy Cross,** Fulham, is a corruption of "Parson's Cross," referring to a cross on the roof of the parsonage on Parson's Green. **Putney** was originally "Puttaney," the Saxon for Putta's Isle; whereas **Wimbledon** was *Wibbandun*, a Celtic term signifying the *dun*, or hill-fort, belonging to one Wibba. The name of

Wandsworth denotes a manor watered by the Wandle. **Lambeth** is a corruption of "Loamhithe,' the Anglo-Saxon for haven of the loamy soil. **Vauxhall** is described in a document dated 1282 as the Manor of Faukeshall. As, however, this manor was originally held by Fulke de Breante soon after the Conquest, it is highly probable that the designation was more correctly *Fulke's Hall*, afterwards corrupted into *Faukeshall*. The present spelling of the name may be traced back to the year 1615, when the Hall, or Manor House, was occupied by Jane Vaux.

Southwark is a modification of the Anglo-Saxon "Suthwerk," and the Danish *Sydrike*, literally the south fortification. During the Danish occupation of England this was a very strong position. **Bermondsey** was anciently written *Beormundsey*, signifying that the *ey*, or strip of land intersected by creeks [*see* CHELSEA, &c.], belonged to Beormund, a prominent Anglo-Saxon lord. **Horselydown** is properly *Horsadown*, so called because this district was originally a down used for grazing horses. **Walworth** was named in honour of Sir William Walworth, Lord Mayor in 1380, who resided here. The **Borough** recalls the fact that the inhabitants of London south of the Thames were *Burghers*, and, therefore, entitled to the rights and privileges of Corporation.

Rotherhithe is Saxon for red haven, alluding to the colour of the soil. The name of **Deptford** indicates the deep ford over the Ravensbourne, which is now spanned by a bridge. **Greenwich** means the green town, or, more precisely, the verdant settlement beside the *wick*, or reach of the river [*see* CHISWICK] ; whereas **Woolwich** was originally *Hylwich*, *i.e.*, hill town. The **Isle of Dogs** is a corruption of " Isle of Ducks," so described in ancient documents on account of the number of wild-fowl always to be found there. **New Cross** derived its name from " The Golden Cross," a famous old coaching-house, rebuilt and renamed " The New Cross." **Lewisham** is properly *Leawreham*, or meadow-home. **Blackheath** is a corruption of *Bleakheath*. **Eltham** was formerly written " Ealdham," the Anglo-Saxon for the old home or dwelling, referring to the palace occupied by the English kings down to the time of James I. **Catford** is a contraction of *Cattleford*, signifying a shallow portion of the Ravensbourne easily forded by cattle. [The University town on the Isis received its present name of OXFORD for a similar reason.] **Beckenham** denotes a home beside the beck or brook. Here again the Ravensbourne comes into notice. **Sydenham** means the home or habitation in the south, The names of **Forest Hill, Norwood,** a contraction of Northwood, and **Westwood** remind us that the whole of this district was formerly a large tract of wooded land. **Dulwich** is a corruption of *Dalewich*, the town in the dale. **Honor Oak** owes its designation to the boundary oak, under whose umbrageous shade Queen Elizabeth is said to have dined. **Nunhead** derived its name from " The

Nuns' Head," a place of holiday resort for Londoners, dating back more than two hundred years. **Peckham** was originally *Beckham,* a home distinguished for its becks or brooks. **Brixton** is a corruption of the Anglo-Saxon "Brigestan," the bridge of stone. **Camberwell** derived its name from a miraculous well discovered close by the parish church dedicated to St. Giles, the patron of cripples. *Cam* is Celtic for crooked. In this instance the word applies to the cripples, or rather to their patron saint. [On the other hand, the University town of CAMBRIDGE was so called from the bridge over the CAM, a river distinguished for its winding course.] **Stockwell** is in allusion to the well found in the *stoc*, or wooded place, in Anglo-Saxon times. **Kennington** means a settlement in the King's meadow. One of the palaces of Henry VIII. stood here. **Newington** denotes the new town in the meadow. Finally, the name of **St. George's Fields** was derived from the neighbouring church of St. George the Martyr.

BATTLES.

THE **Tearless Victory** was the name given by Plutarch to the victory won by Archimadus, King of Sparta, over the Argives and Arcadians in the year 367 B.C. without the loss of a single Spartan soldier. **The Thundering Legion** is the historical designation given to the Roman legion that overthrew the Alemanni in the year 179 A.D., during a thunderstorm, which was supposed to have been sent in answer to the prayers offered up by the Christians. Not only did the storm strike terror into the minds of their enemies, but it also enabled the Romans to relieve their long-protracted thirst. **The Hallelujah Victory** received its name from the battle-cry of the newly-baptized Bretons, who were led to the attack by Germanus, Bishop of Auxerre, in the year 429.

The Battle of the Standard, fought between the English and the Scots at Northallerton, August 29, 1138, was so called because the standard of the former consisted of a tall crucifix borne upon a wagon. From the crucifix itself there was suspended the Consecrated Host enclosed in a pyx, while floating beneath were the bannerets of SS. Peter, Wilfrid, and John of Beverley. **The Battle of the Herrings** (Feb-

ruary 12, 1429) obtained its title from the defeat
suffered by the Duc de Bourbon when attempting to
intercept a convoy of salted herrings on their way
to the English besieging Orleans. **The Battle of
Spurs** is the more familiar designation of the Battle
of Guinnegate, in which Henry VIII. defeated the
Duc de Longueville (August 16, 1513), because the
French were said to have used their spurs more
than their swords. This event, however, must not
be confounded with **The Battle of the Spurs of
Gold,** which took place between the French and
the Flemish at Courtray, in Belgium, July 11, 1302.
In this engagement the French were completely
routed, and the spurs of upwards of eight thousand
of the vanquished knights were left upon the field.
These were collected and preserved as trophies of
war in the Church of Notre Dame de Courtray.

   The Battle of Marignano (September 13, 1515)
also bears the name of **The Battle of the Giants,**
owing to the defeat by Francis I., King of France, of
1,200 Swiss Guards, the allies of the Milanese. The
Battle of Leipsic (October 16–18, 1813) is known
as **The Battle of All the Nations,** because, in
addition to signalizing the overthrow of Napoleon
and the deliverance of Germany, it was the champion
battle of the nations of Europe.

THAT **New Year's Day** is the first day of the recurring year goes without saying. Previous to 1752, when the year commenced on the 25th of March, its four recognized quarters were Whitsuntide, Lammastide, Martinmastide, and Candlemastide; at the present time they are Lady Day, Midsummer, Michaelmas, and Christmas. Let us at once consider the meaning of these terms.

Whitsuntide is the season ushered in by **Whit Sunday,** a corruption of **White Sunday,** because, during the primitive ages of the Church, all newly-baptized persons were required to attend Mass in white garments on this day. As every one knows, Whit Sunday commemorates the descent of the Holy Spirit upon the Apostles in the form of fiery tongues. It is highly probable, therefore, that the true meaning of Whit, or White, Sunday remains to be sought in connection with the wisdom symbolized by these fiery tongues. After all, the original spelling of this festival-name may have been Witan Sunday, the Anglo-Saxon for Wisdom Sunday; just as the earliest English parliaments were styled WITANAGEMOTES, or "meetings of the wise men." But to proceed. **Lammastide** literally signified the season of First

Fruits; since on **Lammas Day,** a term compounded
out of the Anglo-Saxon *hlaf,* a loaf, and *mæsse,* a
feast, (Aug. 1st), it was formerly the custom to offer
bread made of new wheat in the churches.   **Martin-
mas Day** (Nov. 4th), latterly corrupted into **Martle-
mas Day,** denotes the Feast of St. Martin, Bishop
of Tours in the fourth century.   **Candlemas Day,**
or the **Feast of the Purification** (Feb. 2nd),
which commemorates the presentation of the Infant
in the Temple in accordance with the Jewish Law
instituted 1490 B.C., because the early Christians
walked in procession to Mass with lighted candles in
their hands on this day.   This religious observance
was introduced by Pope Gelasius in the fifth century,
as a literal bearing out of the words spoken by Holy
Simeon when he took the child Jesus in his arms :
' Lord, now lettest Thou Thy servant depart in peace,
according to Thy word ; For mine eyes have seen Thy
salvation, which Thou hast prepared before the face
of all people : *A light to lighten the Gentiles,* and the
glory of Thy people Israel " (*Luke* ii. 29-32).   It is
still the practice in the Roman Catholic Church to
make offerings of candles for the use of the altar on
this day.   **Lady Day** (Mar. 25th) is but another
name for the **Feast of the Annunciation,** or the
day upon which "the angel of the Lord appeared unto
Mary," and announced that she was to become the
Mother of the Son of God.   **Midsummer Day** (June
24th) expresses the midday of the year; while **Michaelmas Day** (Sept. 29th) is the Feast of St. Michael,
the patron saint of the Roman Catholic Church.   As

the latter feast falls upon the first day of autumn, the hiring of labourers and domestics in the rural districts takes place at this time. **Christmas Day** is, to put it literally, the Feast Day of Christ, being the anniversary of the Nativity of the Blessed Redeemer.

Innocents' Day, formerly known as **Childermas Day** (Dec. 28th), commemorates the Massacre of the Innocents by Herod. **Twelfth Day** (Jan. 6th), signifying the twelfth day after Christmas Day, bears the ecclesiastical name of the **Epiphany,** from the Greek *Epiphaneia,* a showing or appearance, because on this day the Infant manifested Himself to the Three Wise Men from the East who came to adore Him. In olden times the Feast of the Epiphany was kept with great solemnity in the churches during the day, followed by a festival of a more social character in the evening, thus accounting for the old-fashioned appellation of **Twelfth Night.** The 7th of January was formerly called **Distaff's Day,** because the Christmas festivities having come to an end with Twelfth Night, the women were expected to return to their distaffs and other regular occupations on this day. Another name for the same occasion was **Rock Day,** *rock* being the Anglo-Saxon term for a distaff. Similarly, the first Monday after the Epiphany bore the designation of **Plough Monday,** on account of the men returning to the plough and the ordinary labours of the field on this day. **Handsel Monday,** the first Monday in the New Year, was so called by the Anglo-Saxons because then it was that *handsels,* or presents, were bestowed upon domestics and children. To the best of our knowledge the custom no longer exists in any portion of this country; or perhaps it may be more correct to say that its observance has been universally transferred to **Boxing Day** (Dec. 26th), originally so styled from the opening of the various alms-boxes in the churches, and the distribution of their contents, which bore the name of a **Christmas Dole,** to the poor by the clergy on this day. Moreover, since heads of families usually gave their children and domestics small sums of money to drop into the boxes for the latter purpose on Christmas morning, we here trace the origin of the term **Christmas Box,** which nowadays applies to a present received by servants and others during the Christmas season.

The word **Lent** is a contraction of the Old English *lenten,* and the Anglo-Saxon *lencten,* the spring, both derived from *lencgan,* to lengthen, because the long fast of the Christian Church occurs when the days begin to lengthen. **Shrove Tuesday,** also known as **Pancake Tuesday,** derived its name from the shriving or confessing imposed upon the faithful on this day. The custom of eating pancakes originated from the fact that this species of food afforded a stay to the appetite during the long hours of waiting in church to be shrived. The distribution of ashes on **Ash Wednesday** commemorates the passage in the third chapter of *Genesis,* where the Lord curses Adam in these words: " In the sweat of thy face thou shalt eat bread till thou return to the ground ; for dust thou art, and unto dust thou shalt return." **Passion Sunday,** which precedes Palm Sunday, is devoted to a general commemoration of the subject of Christ's Passion. **Palm Sunday** owes its name to the distribution of palms in the Roman Catholic Church, in allusion to the palms borne by the populace who accompanied the Redeemer into Jerusalem shortly before His betrayal by Judas. The week following Palm Sunday is called **Passion Week,** and also **Holy Week,** because it contains the days upon which the incidents of Christ's Passion are particularly commemorated. **Maunday Thursday** is the first, not at all on account of the *maund,* the Saxon term for an alms-basket, formerly presented to the poor by the Lord (or rather by the Lady, "the loaf-giver") of the Manor, but from the ancient ceremony of washing the feet of poor persons, in imitation of Christ at the Last Supper, when He said, "Mandatum novum do vobis," &c., the French for *Mandatum* being *Maundé.* The ecclesiastical designation of this day is **Holy Thursday,** in commemoration of the Agony and Bloody Sweat of the Saviour in the Garden of Gethsemane **Good Friday,** the anniversary of the Crucifixion, was originally known as "God's Friday." The Anglo-Saxons usually called this day **Long Friday,** in consequence of the length of the Church service. **Holy Saturday** is the day upon which the Church commemorates the Burial of Christ.

The word **Easter** bears in itself no Christian significance whatever, having been derived from

Eoster, the goddess of light, or spring, in whose honour a festival was anciently held in the month of April. The Jewish festival corresponding to our Easter is called the **Passover,** in commemoration of the Destroying Angel having *passed over* the houses of the Israelites whose door-posts were marked with the blood of a lamb killed the previous night in accordance with the Divine command, when He smote the firstborn of the Egyptians in the year 1491 B.C. Returning to the Christian Church, the Sunday after Easter is called **Low Sunday,** because it stands at the bottom of the Lenten Calendar; being the last day upon which Roman Catholics may fulfil their Easter obligation of receiving the Holy Communion. **Sexagesima Sunday, Quinquagesima Sunday,** and **Quadragesima Sunday** are situated in the Calendar respectively sixty, fifty, and forty days before Easter; the terms expressing the Latin for those round numbers.

The Feast of Whitsuntide, which we have already discussed, also bears the name of **Pentecost,** from the Greek *pentekoste,* the fiftieth day, in commemoration of the gift of the Law to the Israelites fifty days after their deliverance out of Egypt. **Trinity Sunday,** so called from the Latin *trinitas,* three, is the Festival of the Holy Trinity, *i.e.,* the unity of the three persons, the Father, the Son, and the Holy Ghost, under one Godhead. **Corpus Christi** expresses the Latin for the Body of Christ, especially alluding to the Last Supper. As the Church considered it out of keeping with the solemnity peculiar

to Holy Week, the celebration of this High Festival
has been transferred to the Thursday after Trinity
Sunday. The Sunday preceding Ascension Day is
called **Rogation Sunday** because it ushers in the
three **Rogation Days,** or days of preparation, conformably to the Latin *rogare,* to beseech, for the
Feast of the Ascension. We may conveniently add
here that **Ember Days** are those days of especial
fasting and prayers that occur in each of the four
seasons of the year, viz., the Wednesday, Thursday,
and Saturday after the first Sunday in Lent, and the
corresponding three days after the Feast of Whitsuntide, the 14th of September, and the 13th of
December. The weeks in which these days occur
are styled **Ember Weeks;** the allusion to embers
(Anglo-Saxon, *æmyrie,* hot ashes) being commemorative of the ancient custom of doing penance by the
wearing of sackcloth and ashes.

On **Ascension Day** the Church celebrates the
Ascension of our Saviour; while the **Feast of the
Assumption** similarly reminds Roman Catholics of
the consummation of the Virgin's mission upon earth
by being assumed into Heaven. **Holy Cross Day,
Holy Rood Day,** and the **Feast of the Exalta-
tion of the Cross** are one and the same, the term
Rood being Old English, derived from the Anglo-
Saxon *rôd,* for cross. This festival, which occurs on
the 14th of September, celebrates the restoration of
the Holy Cross of Calvary to Jerusalem in the year
628. **All Saints' Day** (Nov. 1st), is the day dedicated to those whose sanctification during life merited

their canonization by the Church after death ; while **All Souls' Day** (Nov. 2nd) is the day set apart for special prayers, having for their object the liberation of the suffering souls in Purgatory.   The older designation of the first-named was **Allhallowes Day,** in accordance with the Anglo-Saxon word *haligan,* holy. **Allhallowe'en** denoted the evening before, generally attended with sundry amusements in the social circle; conspicuous among which was the cracking of nuts in large quantities in the fire, whence it received the name of **Cracknut Night.**

   St. Valentine's Day (Feb. 14th) is sacred to the memory of Bishop Valentine, a Christian martyr beheaded at Rome on this day in the year 278.   The custom among young people of sending poetical souvenirs to their sweethearts on the birthday of St. Valentine originated from the old notion that birds commenced to couple on this day : hence, a sweetheart chosen on the 14th of February anciently bore the name of a VALENTINE.   Nowadays, alas ! the paper VALENTINES are all that remain to remind us of the fact.   **St. Swithin's Day** (July 15th) perpetuates the memory of St. Swithin, the preceptor of King Ethelwulf and Bishop of Winchester, who died July 2, 862.   The vulgar belief that if it rains on this day it will continue to rain for forty successive days is attributed to the tradition that when, despite the saint's dying request to be buried in the churchyard, the clergy took steps to disinter his body in order to remove it within the cathedral, a heavy downpour of rain necessitated a postponement of

their efforts on thirty-nine successive days, whereupon, after the fortieth attempt, they determined to
allow the saint to remain where he lay.   **St. David's
Day** (Mar. 1st) commemorates the victory won by
the Welsh over the Saxons on the birthday of their
Archbishop (born 490, died 554), in the year 540.   It
was in consequence of the Archbishop having ordered
them on this occasion to place a leek in their caps, so
as to distinguish one another from the invaders, that
the Welsh afterwards adopted the leek as their
national emblem in his honour. **Comb's Mass,**
which in the north of Scotland, and Caithness more
particularly, takes the place of our Whitsuntide, is
the colloquial term for the Feast of St. Columba,
Abbot of Iona (born 521, died 597).

Primrose Day (April 19th) is the anniversary of
the death of Lord Beaconsfield (born 1804, died 1881).
The abundant display of primroses on this day, particularly on the part of the members of the Primrose
League, established in 1884 in his honour, originated
in the Queen's primrose wreath sent to the funeral of
the great statesman, thus inscribed—" His favourite
flower."   The custom of displaying a sprig of oak on
Royal Oak Day (May 29th) perpetuates the manner
in which the Royalists welcomed the return to England of Charles II. on his birthday, May 29, 1651,
in allusion to his concealment in the oak at Boscobel,
after the Battle of Worcester, on the 3rd of September previous. **Guy Fawkes' Day** keeps alive the
incident of the Gunpowder Plot, by the timely discovery of which, November 5, 1605, the wholesale

destruction of King James's Parliament was averted.
The name of the chief conspirator was not Guy, but
Guido Fawkes; his execution took place January 13,
1606.

Arbor Day is an expression scarcely understood
in this country, except, perhaps, at Newcastle-upon-
Tyne, where the Transatlantic ceremony of planting
trees, shrubs, and flowers within the school precincts,
was publicly performed for the first time by the Mayor,
June 11, 1888.   This annual observance prevails not
only throughout the United States and Canada, but
also in certain portions of British Columbia, where
the trees have to be coaxed into growing.   **Forefathers' Day** (Dec. 20th) is kept as a high holiday
in New England, commemorative of the landing of
the Pilgrim Fathers at New Plymouth in the year
1620.   **Independence Day** (July 4th), perpetuates
the memory of the American Declaration of Independence, 1776; and **Evacuation Day** (Nov. 25th),
the date of the evacuation of New York City by the
British army, at the conclusion of the American
War of Independence, 1783.

The Sunday in Mid-Lent when the Pope blesses
the Golden Rose, and children and domestics out at
service visit their mothers to feast upon MOTHERING
CAKES, really owes its name of **Mothering Sunday**
to the ancient custom of making offerings to " Mother
Church " on the afternoon of this day.   **St. Grouse's
Day** is a popular nickname given to the 12th of
August **(Grouse Day)**, when grouse shooting
commences; and **St. Partridge's Day,** to the

1st of September **(Partridge Day),** which opens the season for partridge shooting; while **Sprat Day** (Nov. 9th) is the first day for selling sprats in London. The expression **Red Letter Day,** signifying a past event generally referred to with pleasure, found its origin in the old almanacks, where the Festivals and Saints' Days were printed in red ink and the rest in black. This arrangement still obtains in Roman Catholic countries.

Holiday is a corruption of Holy Day, or a day originally set apart by the Roman Catholic Church for the celebration of some feast in commemoration of an important event, or in honour of a particular saint. The word **Almanac,** also written **Almanack,** is derived from the Arabic *al manah,* to count; whereas **Calendar** is a contraction of the Latin *calendarium,* an account-book.

TEXTILES, EMBROIDERIES, AND LACE.

SEVERAL of our textile fabrics are indebted for their names to the places where they were first manufactured. As examples: **Damask Linens and Silks** originally came from Damascus; **Muslin** from Moosul, in Mesopotamia; **Nankeen** from Nankin, in China; **Calico** from Calicut, on the Malabar Coast; **Cashmere** from the valley of Cashmere, in India; **Dimity** from Damietta, in Egypt; **Valence** from Valencia, in Spain; and **Holland** from the Netherlands. **Cambric** was first made at Cambray; **Shalloon** at Chalons; and **Tarlatan** at Tarare: each of these towns being situated in France. **Worsted** formerly comprised the staple industry of a town of that name in Norfolk; **Cobourg** is brought from Cobourg, in Germany; while **Angola** comes from the Portuguese territory so called on the West Coast of Africa. The coarse woollen cloth known as **Frieze** was originally imported from Friesland.

The name of **Cotton** is a modification of the Arabic *qoton*; **Silk** is derived from the Latin *sericus*, soft; and **Satin** from the Italian *seta*, a species of silk distinguished for its gloss and close texture. Variegated silk or other stuff bears the name of **Brocade** in accordance with the Italian verb *broccare*, to prick, to stitch, to figure; **Damassin** is a damask cloth interwoven with flowers, or silver, or gold; **Sarsanet** is a fine silk, originally made by the Saracens; **Mohair** is properly Moorhair, or the hair of the Angola goat introduced into Spain by the Moors; whereas **Moirè Antique** is the French description of a watered silk worked up in the manner of that worn in the olden time. **Chintz** is a Persian word signifying spotted or stained; **Taffety**, or **Taffeta**, is a modification of the Persian *tâftah*, derived from *taftan*, to spin; **Linen** is an Anglo-Saxon rendering of the Latin *linum*, flax; and **Lawn** is simply fine linen bleached upon a lawn instead of the customary drying-ground. **Pompadour** received its name from Madame le Pompadour, the mistress of Louis XV. of France (born 1721, died 1764), who was the first to introduce it.

Swansdown is, of course, made from the down of swans; **Moleskin** is not the skin of the mole, but a strong cotton fabric or fustain having a smooth surface like the mole-skin; **Merino** is manufactured from the wool of the Merino sheep; and **Alpaca** from that of the alpaca, a species of *llama* found in Peru. **Kersey** is a corruption of **Jersey**, indicative of the place where this favourite woollen material was first produced. The dyed cotton stuff known as **Gingham**, out of which umbrellas were formerly made—hence the slang term for those articles—is so called after the native Javanese name pronounced *ginggang*. We may also conveniently add here that **Blankets** received their designation from Thomas Blanket, who first made them at Bristol as long ago as the year 1340.

The name of **Velvet** traces its origin from the Latin *villus*, shaggy hair ; and **Plush** from *pilus*, a hair. **Velveteen** is a cotton velvet or a cloth in imitation of velvet. **Fustian,** derived from the Spanish *fustan*, is a generic term for the twilled cotton stuffs of which velvet, corduroy, &c., are the chief. **Grogram** is a corruption of the French *gros-grain*, meaning coarse-grained ; whereas **Corduroy** is properly *Cord du roy*, King's Cord, so called because, owing to its ribbed or corded surface, it was at one time considered superior to any other kind of cloth intended for masculine wear. **Pina-cloth,** a material much used for ladies' dresses, is manufactured from the fibres of the pine-apple leaf ; just as **Grass-cloth** is extensively worked up into light jackets for Indian wear from the Grass Cloth plant which abounds in China, Assam, and Sumatra. **T-cloth** comprises a special kind of cloth expressly manufactured in this country for exportation to India, and distinguished by a *T* marked upon it ; while **Broadcloth** simply bears its name on account of its unusual width. The name of **Twill** is a modification of the German *Zwillich*, signifying trellis-work, and founded upon *twillen*, to separate in two, since this cloth presents the appearance of diagonal lines or ribs upon its surface. **Tweed** is a cloth made in the neighbourhood of the river Tweed; but it did not always bear this name. The cloth is really *twill*, and the altered designation arose out of the word being blotted in an invoice sent to James Locke, of London, who, conceiving it to look like "Tweed," suggested that it might as well stand for the name of the cloth as any other. **Plaid** owes its name to the Gaelic *peallaid*, a sheepskin out of which the overgarments of the Highlanders were originally made. **Check** is but another name for Plaid, meaning checkered, *i.e.*, marked with variegated or crossed lines; as, for example, a draught-board, of which the counters are, on account of their cross movements, called CHECKERS or CHEQUERS.

The word **Embroidery** is a modern substantive evolved out of the old verb "Embordering," by which was meant the adornment of any material with a border. **Tapestry** is derived, through the French *tapisserie*, from the Latin *tapes*, a carpet. The celebrated **Bayeaux Tapestry,** supposed to have been the work of Matilda, queen of William the Conqueror, and her maidens, took its name from the Norman town where it was discovered in 1728. **Gobelin Tapestry** preserves the memory of the Brothers Gobelin, the great French dyers (flourished 1470) whose house in Paris was acquired in 1662 by Louis XIV. for the production of tapestry and other works of ornamental design suitable for the adornment of palaces under the direction of M. Colbert. The more ancient name for Tapestry was that of **Arras,** in allusion to the town situated in the French Netherlands whence it chiefly came.

Having regard to Lace, it will suffice to observe that **Lisle, Chantilly, Brussells, Honiton,** &c., severally identify the Lace with the local centres where its manufacture is principally carried on ; that **Valenciennes** is made at Valenciennes, in France ; and that **Colbertine** derives its name from M. Colbert, the superintendent of the French Royal Lace Factories established by Louis XIV. in the seventeenth century. Lace is styled **Point-lace** when it is worked with the point of a needle ; and **Pillow-lace** when produced by twisted threads around a series of pins arranged on a cushion. The latter, which has so greatly superseded the more costly point-lace, is said to have been the invention of Barbara Uttmann, of St. Annaberg, in the year 1561. The word **Lace** itself comes from the Latin *laques,* a noose or snare. **Tulle,** a species of network or lace, is indebted for its designation to the French town of that name where it was first made.

LITERARY PSEUDONYMS.

SO far from being chosen at random these are frequently the result of much premeditation. **Voltaire** (born 1694, died 1778), whose proper name was Arovet, composed out of this and the initials L. I. (*le jeune*) the anagram by which all his writings are identified. Again, **Barry Cornwall** is an imperfect anagram founded upon Bryan Waller Procter (born 1790, died 1874), the poet's real name; whereas **Yendys,** the signature of Sydney Dobell (born 1824, died 1874), was merely the Christian name reversed. To cite an instance of another class: Charles James Apperley, of Denbighshire, author of "The Chase, the Turf, and the Road," and a regular contributor to *The Quarterly Review* could scarcely have hit upon a more fitting pseudonym than that of **Nimrod,** who "was a mighty hunter before the Lord," alluded to in *Genesis* x. 9. Such a choice will be the better understood, perhaps, when it is mentioned that out of regard for the sporting tastes of his esteemed contributor, Mr. Pittman, the proprietor of the *Quarterly* kept a stud of hunters for his especial use. Equally appropriate was the pseudonym **Zadkiel,** denoting the angel of the planet Jupiter, adopted by Lieutenant Richard James Morrison, author of "The Prophetic Almanack," which still survives as an annual publication.

Washington Irving selected the *nom de plume* of **Knickerbocker** for his "History of New York," in allusion to the wide breeches worn by the original settlers of that city. The true account of how Charles Lamb (born 1775, died 1834) adopted the name of **Elia** for his "Essays" is as follows:— His first contribution to the "London Magazine" being a description of the Old South Sea House, in which he had spent several months of his noviciate as a clerk, he at the very moment of appending his signature, bethought himself of a gay, light-hearted foreigner who used to flutter about there ; and, as a mere matter of whim, he wrote down the name of that individual instead of his own. **Boz,** the early *nom de plume* of Charles Dickens (born 1812, died 1870), arose out of the nickname of Moses conferred by him upon a younger pet brother in honour of Moses Primrose in the "Vicar of Wakefield." The other children of the family, however, found it impossible to utter a nearer pronunciation to the name than "Bozes," which presently became shortened in "Boz"; and the latter hit the fancy of our young author sufficiently to lead him to its adoption at that period of his literary career when he lacked the confidence to appear before the world under his own name. Out of an analogous incident sprang **Ouida,** the pseudonym of one of the most widely-read lady novelists of the present day. Her actual name is Louise de la Ramée (born in 1840) ; but remarking the infantile conversion of Louise into " Ouida," she was struck by the novelty of such a *nom de plume*, and immediately adopted it. Another lady novelist of probably higher attainments assumed the name of **George Sand** (born 1804, died 1876) as the outcome of her attachment to a young student named Jules Sand, or rather Sandeau, with whom she collaborated in the production of " Rose et Blanche," her first novel. The real name of this lady was Mdlle. Dupin, afterwards changed by marriage to Madame Dudevant.

It may be deemed interesting to learn also that **Artemus Ward** was an actual name borne by an eccentric showman with whom Charles Farrar Browne, the American humorist (born 1834, died 1867) often came into personal contact ; and, further, that Samuel Langhorne Clemens (born in 1835) owes his singular pseudonym to the fact of having been employed in early life as a pilot on one of the Mississippi River steamboats. The nautical phrase for taking soundings, **Mark Twain,** or, in other words, " mark two fathoms," suggested the name under which the works of the latter have become widely popular on both sides of the Atlantic.

Finally, not every one is aware that **F. M. Allen,** the pseudonym of Mr. Edmund Downey, author of "The Voyage of the Ark," "Through Green Glasses," and some other books of Irish humour, was his wife's maiden name.

COUNTERFEIT PRESENTMENTS.

A **PORTRAIT,** so called from the Latin *pro-trahere*, to draw forth, is produced by the individual skill of an artist; whereas a **Photograph,** conformably to the two Greek words *photos*, light, and *graphein*, to write, is obtained by the action of sunlight upon a chemically prepared surface, such as silver, zinc, copper, glass, or paper.

The earliest examples of portraiture were styled **Miniatures** because they originated from the head of the Virgin or of some well-known saint introduced into the initial letters of illuminated rubics by the **Miniatori,** a number of monks noted for their skill in painting with *minium,* or red lead. The reason why the portraits of monarchs are represented on coins and medals in **Profile** dates back to Antigonus, one of the generals of Alexander the Great, who, having lost one eye, ordered his likeness to be drawn from a side view. This occurred in the year 330 B.C. The term is a corruption, by way of the French *profil,* of the Latin *perfilum*, compounded out of *per*, through, by, and *filum,* a line, a thread. A profile cut out of black paper bears the name of a **Silhouette** in honour of Etienne de Silhouette, the French Comptroller of Finance under Louis XV. (born 1709, died 1767), who was the first to have his features outlined in this manner.

The earlier descriptions of photographs were respectively styled **Talbotypes, Daguerreotypes,** and **Ferriertypes,** after the names of their inventors. The smaller-sized photographs at present in use were originally described as **Cartes-de-Visite** from the practice of the Duc de Parma, who, while staying at Nice in the year 1857, had his photograph produced on the back of his visiting cards. The designation **Vignette,** which expresses the French diminutive of vine or tendril, owes its origin to the vine-leaves or branches that properly surround the photographs produced in this style. A photograph of the larger size is called a **Cabinet** because it forms a picture suited to the walls of a cabinet or very small room. A three-quarter-length photograph or portrait is styled among artists a **Kit-Kat,** in allusion to the portraits of the original members of the " Kit-Kat Club," which were painted by Sir Godfrey Kneller for Jacob Tonson, the secretary, to suit the dimensions of the room in which the Club was latterly held at his villa at Barn Elms. Similarly, a canvas measuring 28 inches by 36 inches is styled a **Kit-Kat Canvas** because this was the uniform size of the famous " Kit-Kat Club portraits." We may as well add here that the KIT-KAT CLUB derived its name from Christopher

Kat, a pastrycook of King Street, Westminster, in whose house the thirty noblemen and gentlemen who formed themselves into a Club for the purpose of promoting the Protestant Succession in the year 1703 held their first meetings.

LONDON INNS AND GARDENS.

IN our article on TAVERN SIGNS we confined ourselves to a general survey of the subject; we
now purpose to consider the significance of a
few Inn Signs that are, or were once, peculiar to
London. Commencing with the celebrated **Tabard**,
in Southwark, so dear to the memory of Chaucer
and his Canterbury Pilgrims, that sign was derived
from the rich tunic or mantle of the same name
worn by military nobles over their armour and
emblazoned with heraldic devices. The Tabard
still forms part of the costume of the heralds. **La
Belle Sauvage,** on Ludgate Hill, was, as is evident
from a legal document dated the thirty-first year of
the reign of Henry VI., known both as " Savage's
Inn" and " The Bell and the Hoop." The latter
was the actual sign, representing a bell within a
hoop, of the Inn which was kept by Isabelle
Savage ; and the combination of these two names
resulted in the punning title of "La Belle Sauvage.'
The Swan with Two Necks, in Lad Lane, was
a corruption of " The Swan with Two Nicks." As
most Londoners are aware, it has long been the
custom of the Vintners' Company, in their annual
" swan-upping " expeditions on the Thames, to mark

their swans with a couple of nicks or notches in the
bill, so as to distinguish them from the royal swans,
whose nicks are five in number, viz., two lengthways
and three across on the bill.   That this characteristic mark of the Vintners' Company should have
been chosen for a London Inn Sign is scarcely
extraordinary.

The sign of **The Elephant and Castle,** on the
south side of the river, was adopted from the crest
of the Cutlers' Company, into whose trade ivory,
and consequently elephants' tusks, enters very considerably.   With regard to the " Castle," this was
in mediæval times inseparable from the idea of an
elephant, owing to the part which these huge
animals anciently took in the Punic wars.   Another
" Elephant and Castle " exists in the parish of
St. Pancras, near King's Cross; but this sign
originated from the discovery, in 1714, of the
skeleton of an elephant in the neighbourhood of
Battle Bridge.   A flint-headed spear lay beside the
remains, and from this it is reasonable to conjecture
that the animal must have been killed by the Britons
who were led by Queen Boadicea against the Romans
in the year 61 A.D.

The Horse Shoe, Tottenham Court Road, came
into existence as a sign from the large horse-shoes
nailed up at the entrance of Messrs. Meux's brewery
adjoining.   The shoes are also conspicuous on the
trappings of the dray-horses belonging to that
establishment ; in short, they comprise the trade-
mark of the firm.   **The Blue Posts,** at the corner

of Hanway Street, nearly opposite the "Horse Shoe," arose out of the fancy of an old innkeeper to distinguish his hostelry from all others by causing the chain-posts abutting on the road to be painted blue instead of white, which eccentricity fully served the purpose of a sign. There is another "Blue Posts" in Cork Street, Piccadilly, and yet another in Southampton Buildings, Holborn; but the first-named is the oldest of the three, and therefore the original. **The Black Posts,** Bond Street, may also be regarded as a modified imitation of the example set by the original "Blue Posts." **The Three Chairmen,** at the foot of Hay Hill, Berkeley Square, and **The Running Footman,** in Hayes' Mews, close by, were so denominated from being the resort of gentlemen's servants in the days when SEDAN CHAIRS (these chairs were first made at Sedan, in France, which accounts for their name, exactly as BATH CHAIRS were originally introduced at Bath during the last century, when fashionable invalids flocked to the West of England to drink the Bath and Cheltenham waters) and Running Foot-men preceded the use of private carriages by the wealthy.

The Mother Red Cap, Camden Town, per-petuates the memory of a notorious poisoner known as "Mother Damnable, the Consort of the Devil," who lived at Hungerford Stairs during the period of the Commonwealth. **The Mother Shipton,** Haver-stock Hill, was built at the time when the prophecies of Mrs. Evan Preece, of Glamorganshire, South

Wales, were in everybody's mouth. This old woman was said to have had a son by the devil, whereupon, in return for the sacrifice of her honour, she was accorded the gift of prophecy. When we state that she correctly predicted the deaths of Lord Percy, Wolsey, and other historical personages, the existence of Mother Shipton in this country must be regarded as a time-honoured if not exactly as a well-founded institution. **The Adelaide,** Haverstock Hill, was named in honour of the consort of William IV., and **The York and Albany** after the title of Frederick, the second son of George III.

Jack Straw's Castle, Highbury, as also the celebrated hostelry of the same name on Hampstead Heath, was so called after Jack Straw, one of the leaders in Wat Tyler's insurrection, who pulled down the Priory of the Knights of St. John of Jerusalem at the former place, and whose habitation was a hole formed out of the hill-side on the site of the present Inn at the latter place. The **Spaniards,** Highgate, was originally the private residence of the Spanish Ambassador to James I. **The Whittington Stone,** Highgate Hill, took its sign from the stone upon which the world-famous Dick Whittington sat down to rest the while he listened to the bells of Bow Church pleasantly chiming across the open fields. The stone is still to be seen on the edge of the pavement exactly opposite the public-house.

The sign of **The Thirteen Cantons,** King Street, Golden Square, was adopted in compliment to the thirteen Protestant cantons of Switzerland, and to the numerous natives of that country who at one time took up their residence in the parish of Soho. During the last decade or two the Swiss population has given way in a large degree to French immigrants. **The North Pole,** Wardour Street, dates back to the time when our national interest in Arctic discovery was at its height; exactly in the same manner as **The South Australian,** Hans Place, Chelsea, was established in the year that first witnessed the colonization of Southern Australia.

The World's End, in the King's Road, Chelsea, a favourite house of entertainment during the Restoration period, received its name on account of its distance from town. **The Fulham Bridge,** at Knightsbridge, recalls the original name of the structure which crossed the Westbourne in this neighbourhood (*See* KNIGHTSBRIDGE). **The Devil,** Fleet Street, received its name from its situation, nearly opposite the Church of St. Dunstan, and the traditional account of that saint having seized the Evil One by the nose with a pair of hot pincers. **The Three Nuns,** Aldgate, well serves the purpose of reminding us of the existence of an ancient priory inhabited by the nuns of St. Clare in this neighbourhood (*see* MINORIES). **The White Conduit Tavern,** Islington, occupies the site of the famous old **White Conduit House,** a popular place of resort previous to its demolition in 1849. This was the Conduit which had served the Carthusian Friars with water from ancient times.

The prenomen " white " applied to the house and was derived from the appearance of its exterior. **The Belvedere,** Pentonville Hill, originally contained a small structure on the roof known by this name for sitting under and enjoying the prospect across the fields. The term *Belvidere* is Italian, signifying " a fine prospect," and is equally applicable to a summer arbour and the flat roof of a house. **The Clown Tavern,** St. John Street Road, Clerkenwell, owes its sign to the fact that it was formerly kept by a clown engaged at Sadler's Wells Theatre, in its immediate vicinity. The well-known **Hummuns's Hotel,** generally alluded to as **Hummuns's,** Covent Garden, derived this title from its erection on the site of a *Hummuns,* the Arabic name for a sweating bath, kept by a Mr. Small some time during the seventeenth century.

Reference to the above Inns and Taverns peculiar to London compels us almost to say a few words concerning those popular places of outdoor resort of which we have all read and heard so much. **Sadler's Wells** marks the position of an ancient holy well whose waters were famous for working extraordinary cures. In the year 1683, after having been stopped up since the Reformation, a Mr. Sadler, while digging for gravel in his garden, discovered this well, and thereafter it bore his name. In order to profit by the re-established fame of this well, Sadler converted his residence into a house of entertainment under the title of " Sadler's Musick House." Here were provided tight-rope dancing, conjuring, tumbling, and a variety of other diversions, always accompanied by music. Sixty years later, probably after the death of Mr. Sadler, the property passed into the hands of Mr. Rosoman, who turned it into a theatre, but retained the name of the old proprietor. The present theatre was built by Mrs. Bateman in 1879. **Highbury Barn,** first a small ale and cake house, and afterwards a place of public entertainment, including a theatre, was so called from its occupying the site of a barn-like structure originally belonging to the ancient Priory of the Knights of St. John of Jerusalem, and left standing after the incursion of Jack Straw and his rebellious companions [*see ante,* JACK STRAW'S CASTLE]. **Vauxhall Gardens** derived their title from the Hall, or Manor-house, of Jane Vaux, which they displaced [*see* VAUXHALL]; **Ranelagh Gardens** occupied the site of Ranelagh House, the seat of an Irish nobleman of that title; while **Cremorne Gardens** were named after Thomas Dawson, Lord Cremorne, whose town house and grounds they covered. Whatever may have been the moral character of these places, their removal has had the effect of effacing one phase of Metropolitan amusement entirely; but it has also been instrumental in introducing another—namely, the Music-Halls. The first London music-hall was "The Canterbury," Westminster Bridge Road, which grew out of **The Canterbury Arms,** displaying the arms of the city of Canterbury in the year 1848.

13

SOBRIQUETS AND NICKNAMES.

THE list of historical personages whose sobriquets and nicknames are even better known than their proper names is very large ; we must, therefore, content ourselves with a random selection of the principal.

Commencing with the ladies : Ayesha (born 610, died 677), the second and favourite wife of Mahomet, was called **The Mother of Believers** because the prophet styled himself " The Father of Believers." **Fair Helen** was the wife of Menelaos, King of Sparta, by whose guest, Paris, the Trojan prince, she was carried off. This incident was the immediate cause of the famous siege of Troy which lasted ten years. **Fair Rosamond** (died 1154) was the mistress of Henry II., who kept her in a secluded bower that could be approached only by a labyrinth or maze in the neighbourhood of the royal palace at Woodstock. One day, however, the queen artfully discovered her way thereto by means of a silken thread attached to the garment of the faithless husband, after which she soon procured the removal of her rival by poison. Joan, the wife of Edward the Black Prince, was styled **The Fair Maid of Kent** (died 1385) on account of her beauty and being the only daughter of the Earl of Kent. **The Holy Maid of Kent** was Elizabeth Barton, a religious enthusiast, hanged at Tyburn in 1534. A brave, if not a beautiful, woman of historic renown was the Countess of Dunbar and March, who, in the year 1337, completely defied the attempt of the Earl of Salisbury to capture Dunbar Castle during a siege of nineteen weeks, at the end of which the latter was forced to retire with ignominy. This warlike heroine is generally alluded to under the name of **Black Agnes,** in consequence of her swarthy complexion. A less fortunate Scottish heroine who fell at the Battle of Ancrum Moor beside her English adversary, General Evers, whom she had killed, was **Fair Maiden Lilliard.** She was buried on the site of the conflict; and her epitaph, as follows, is known to every man, woman, and child in that part of the country :—

> " Fair Maiden Lilliard lies under this stene,
> Little was her stature, but great was her fame ;
> Upon the English loons she laid many thumps,
> And when her legs were cutted off, she fought upon her
>   stumps."

The spot where she fell still bears the name of " Lilliard's Edge." Then, of course, we have the celebrated Joan of Arc, **The Maid of Orleans** (born 1412, burnt at the stake 1431), who placed herself at the head of the attacking party and effected the capture of the city of Orleans from the English. Neither must we omit a passing allusion to Augustine Zaragossa, better known as **The Maid of Saragossa,** owing to the signal heroism which she displayed during the siege of her native city in 1808-9. The Honourable Elizabeth St. Leger, the niece of Colonel Anthony St. Leger, who founded the Stakes named after him in connection with Doncaster races, is known to posterity as **The Lady Freemason,** because on one occasion she overheard the proceedings of an assembly of Freemasons, and, being discovered, was, as the only way of meeting an unprecedented difficulty, duly elected a member of the craft and initiated into its peculiar rites and ceremonies. Madame Jenny Lind Goldschmidt (born 1821, died 1887) was styled **The Swedish Nightingale** on account of her vocal genius and her birth in the city of Stockholm. The now popular society actress, Mrs. Langtry, bears the somewhat punning though highly complimentary sobriquet of **The Jersey Lily,** because she was born in Jersey and her Christian name is Lillie.

Heraclitus of Ephesus (flourished 500 B.C.) was known as **The Weeping Philosopher,** because he spent the latter years of his life in grieving over the folly of men; on the other hand, Democritus of Abdera (born 460 B.C., died 357 B.C.) merited the surname of **The Laughing Philosopher,** because he jeered at the feeble powers of man, whose every act was in the hands of fate. Duns Scotus, the Scottish schoolman (born 1272, died 1308), was styled **The Subtle Doctor** by reason of his learning; while St. Thomas Aquinas (born 1227, died 1274) was denominated **The Angelic Doctor** because he belonged to the priesthood. **St. Paul of the Cross** is the name by which Paul Francis (born 1694, died 1775), founder of the religious Order of the Passionists, is best known.

The famous English outlaw who flourished between the years 1180 and 1247, and whose real name was Robert Fitz-ooth, Earl of Huntingdon, adopted the style of **Robin Hood,** in deference to the example set by the people of Nottinghamshire, who, while dropping the *Fitz*, corrupted the *Robert* into Robin and the *ooth* into Hood. **Little John** was properly called John Little, but being a great, stalwart fellow, the outlaw chief took a fancy to invert his name for the sake of the contrast. We can quite understand "the merry men of Sherwood Forest" cultivating an objection to hard-sounding words; therefore it could not have been long before William Scathelocke, another prominent member of Robin Hood's band, found his name reduced to the more euphonious form of **Will Scarlet.** **Friar Tuck** was so called because his habit was *tucked in* around the waist by a girdle.

Sixteen-string Jack was the name popularly bestowed upon Jack Rann, a notorious highwayman hanged in 1791, owing to the sixteen tags he wore on his breeches, eight at each knee. Another notorious representative of the great family of Jacks, good, bad, and otherwise, was the Marquis of Waterford, commonly known as **Spring-heel Jack,** from his habit of frightening people by springing upon them out of obscure corners after nightfall during the early part of the present century. **Gentleman Jack** and **Gentleman Smith** were the titles respectively borne by John Bannister and William Smith, both actors of the century gone by. The former was noted for his straightforward dealings with his fellow-men in private life, the latter for his gentlemanly deportment on the stage.

Who has not heard of **Admirable Crichton?** This extraordinary Scottish prodigy, James Crichton (born 1560, died 1583), is said to have given such early proofs of his learning that the degree of Master of Arts was conferred upon him at the age of fourteen. In addition to his classical knowledge, he was a poet, a musician, a sculptor, an artist, an actor, a brilliant conversationalist, a good horseman, and an excellent fencer. Surely the possessor of such varied accomplishments deserved a better fate than that which befell him in the very prime of his life! He was stabbed by a band of masked desperadoes led by his own pupil, Vincenzo Gonzaga, the son of the Duke of Mantua. A genius of a totally different stamp was George Robert Fitzgerald, better known, owing to his duelling proclivities, as **Fighting Fitzgerald.** This individual was one of the most infamous characters of the last century. No enemy ever escaped him with life; being a sure shot and an expert swordsman, his intense love of gambling and duelling, united to a haughty and overbearing disposition, habitually prompted him to shed the blood of his fellow-men without the least compunction.

A celebrated leader of fashion during the early part of this century was Robert Coates, popularly styled **Romeo Coates** in consequence of his fondness for playing the part of Romeo at amateur theatricals. Among other past notabilities of fashion we may mention **Beau Fielding, Beau Brummell,** and **Beau Nash,** severally so styled from the foppishness of their attire. The last-named (born 1674, died 1761) was a notorious diner-out, and for some time Master of the Ceremonies at the fashionable Assembly Rooms at Bath, where he provided a series of entertainments the like of which had never been known. On this account he was surnamed **King of Bath.** Alas! though literally the "monarch of all he surveyed" during the brief period of his popularity, when at length Death claimed him for his own he was as poor as the meanest of King George's subjects.

But Richard "Beau" Nash was not the only British subject who has rejoiced in the erstwhile title of King. As examples: Richard Oastler, of Bradford (born 1789, died 1861), merited the style of **The Factory King,** in recognition of his success in promoting the "Ten Hours' Bill"; George Hudson, of Yorkshire (born 1800, died 1871), chairman of the Midland Railway Company, was denominated **The Railway King,** because in one day he cleared the large sum of £100,000 by fortunate railway speculations; John Law, the projector of the Mississippi Scheme (born 1671, died 1729), bore the name of **The Paper King,** than which, by the way, nothing could have

been more appropriate. The huge fortunes antici-
pated by the subscribers to this wholesale fraud
appeared promising enough upon paper, or, to put it
more precisely, in the prospectus; but hard cash
there was none, saving such as passed into the pockets
of the wily promoter. In our own decade we have
The Nitrate King, the sobriquet of Colonel J. T.
North, of Eltham, consequent upon his successful
speculations in the commodity with which his name
has become associated.

John Kyrle, of Ross, Herefordshire (born 1637,
died 1754), well known for his artistic tastes and acts
of benevolence, was styled by Pope **The Man of
Ross,** because he was constantly effecting improvements for the public good in the neighbourhood of
his estate. Another local philanthropist was Dr.
William Gordon, of Hull (born 1801, died 1849),
whose surname, **The People's Friend,** so well
merited during life, literally followed him to the
grave, where it appears chiselled on his tombstone.
Perhaps the greatest benefactor of the human race
with whom we have become practically acquainted
in modern times, was Father Mathew (born 1790,
died 1856), universally styled **The Apostle of
Temperance,** beside whom, judging from results,
all our latter-day temperance advocates sink into
insignificance. He was also made the recipient of
the sobriquet **The Sinner's Friend,** on account of
the special interest he took in the fallen and the
outcast; even the most degraded always met with a
welcome at his hands.

The Musical Small-coal Man was the popular
designation of Thomas Britton (born 1650, died
1714), a vendor of small coals, which he carried in a
sack over his shoulder and cried in the streets, who
on Thursday evenings gave a series of high-class
instrumental concerts in the room over his shed in
Clerkenwell, assisted by the best talent he could
procure, that attracted all fashionable London. This
gifted person was actually frightened to death by the
freak of a ventriloquist. Thomas Rawlinson, the
bibliopolist (born 1681, died 1725), was appropriately enough styled **Tom Folio.** **The Infant
Roscius** (born 1791, died 1874) was William Henry
Betty, a histrionic prodigy named after the greatest
actor of antiquity. His *début* took place at Belfast,
August 19, 1803; and three months later he appeared
at Covent Garden (then under the management of
the elder Macready) for twelve nights at a salary of
fifty guineas a night and a clear benefit. During
this brief season the public excitement was so great
that the military had to be called out every night to
preserve order. His last appearance as a boy-actor
occurred at Bath in the year 1808.

William Gerard Hamilton, the Irish Chancellor
of the Exchequer (born 1729, died 1756), has been
handed down to posterity under the name of
Single-speech Hamilton, because he delivered but
one speech in the House, and that was such a mar-
vellous outburst of rhetoric that it electrified all who
heard it. This memorable incident took place
November 13, 1755. Henry Dundas, afterwards

Lord Melville (born 1740, died 1811), merited the sobriquet of **Starvation Dundas** in consequence of his repeated use of the word "starvation" in the course of a debate on American affairs in the year 1775. Sir Robert Peel (born 1750, died 1830), during the time he was Chief Secretary for Ireland (1812 to 1816), was popularly denominated **Orange Peel,** on account of his strong anti-Catholic spirit [*see* ORANGEMEN]. William Pitt, Earl of Chatham (born 1708, died 1778), was styled **The Heaven-sent Minister** because the most splendid triumphs of British arms were achieved during his administration. John Russell, afterwards created Earl Russell (born 1792, died 1878), received the nickname of **Finality John** from the fact of his maintaining that the Reform Bill of 1832 was a *finality*. The late Earl of Beaconsfield (born 1804, died 1881) owed his popular name of **Dizzy** to his own habit of setting forth his early novels during the lifetime of his father under the authorship of " D'Israeli the Younger." In course of time this became shortened into " Dizzy," and it clung to him ever afterwards.

Mr. W. E. Gladstone (born 1809) first received the nickname of **The Grand Old Man** on the occasion of the unseating in the House of Commons of Mr. Charles Bradlaugh (June 1880), through his refusal to take the oath after his election as member for Northampton. At this time Mr. Bradlaugh found a strong champion in Mr. Labouchere ; and the nickname arose out of the latter's conversation in the tea-room of the House "I told some friends," said Mr. Labouchere, referring to the incident of Mr. Bradlaugh's expulsion, "that before I left Mr. Gladstone came to me, and that *grand old man*, with tears in his eyes, took me by the hands and said, 'Mr. Labouchere, bring me Mr. Bradlaugh back again.'"

Mr. William Henry Smith, M.P., the present First Lord of the Treasury (born 1825), is popularly known by the name of **Bookstall Smith** because he originated the idea of railway bookstalls, and founded the now widely-popular firm of "W. H. Smith and Sons."

Sir Christopher Hatton (born 1540, died 1591) was styled **The Dancing Chancellor** because he first attracted the notice of Queen Elizabeth by his graceful dancing at one of the Court masques. In recognition of this accomplishment he was created a Knight of the Garter and subsequently made Chancellor of England. **Praise-God Barebones,** or, rather, Barebon, who died in 1680, was a leather-seller and the leader of the celebrated "Barebones Parliament." It was a common custom among the Puritans to nickname people in accordance with their habits and peculiarities; consequently this individual must have been addicted to praising God in the hearing of his neighbours. William Huntingdon, the preacher and theologian (born 1744, died 1813), called himself **Sinner-saved Huntingdon** for reasons doubtless best known to himself. **Orator Henley,** otherwise John Henley (born 1692, died 1756), was an English divine who in 1726 delivered a course of lectures on theological subjects on Sundays, and on secular subjects on Wednesdays, in a kind of " oratory " or chapel in Newport Market, which attracted large congregations.

Memory Woodfall was the sobriquet of William Woodfall (born 1745, died 1803), brother to the reputed author of the famous " Letters of Junius." This person's memory was so perfect that he was able, after listening to a Parliamentary debate, to report it the next morning word for word without the assistance of any notes whatever. Of another kind was the memory possessed by John Thompson, the son of a greengrocer in the parish of St. Giles, popularly known as **Memory-corner Thompson** (born 1757, died 1843) on account of his astounding local knowledge. Within twenty-four hours, and at two sittings, he drew entirely from memory a correct plan of the parish of St. James's. This plan contained all the squares, streets, lanes, courts, passages, markets, churches, chapels, houses, stables, and angles of houses, in addition to a number of minor objects, such as walls, trees, &c., and including an exact plan of Carlton House and St. James's Palace. He also, on another occasion, made a correct plan of St. Andrew's parish, and offered to do the same with the parishes of St. Giles, St. Paul's, Covent Garden, and St. Clement-Danes. If a particular house in any given street were named, he would tell at once what trade was carried on in it, the appearance and position of the shop, and its contents. In going through a large hotel completely furnished,

he was able to retain a recollection of everything he
saw, and afterwards make an inventory of the whole.
But, perhaps more wonderful than all, he could,
after having read a newspaper overnight, repeat any
desired portion of its contents *verbatim* the next
morning. Nowadays such a one would be exhibited
at the Royal Aquarium as a natural curiosity.

Another well-known London character was **Dirty
Dick,** otherwise Nathaniel Bentley, the miser, who
never washed himself. This extraordinary individual
died in the odour of dirt in the year 1809, leaving an
ample fortune to console his heirs for his loss (?).
The house which he inhabited in Bishopsgate Street
Without has now been converted into a modern wine
and spirit establishment, under the style of THE
D.D. CELLARS. Laurence Brown, the English landscape gardener (born **1715,** died **1783**) was nicknamed
Capability Brown owing to his habitual use of
the word *capability*. At the present day the Duke
of Cambridge (born **1819**) is usually denominated
George Ranger in allusion to his appointment as
Ranger of the Royal Parks. Ernest Benzon, author
of " How I Lost £250,000 in Two Years," rejoiced
in the title of **The Jubilee Plunger** because he
entered upon his gambling career in 1887, the Jubilee
year of Queen Victoria [*see* PLUNGER].

A few of the more celebrated painters may now
detain us. Peter Aartsen, the Flemish painter (born
1507, died 1573), bore the name of **Long Peter** on
account of his extraordinary height ; while Gaspar
Smitz, the Dutch portrait painter (died 1689), was

styled **Magdalen Smith** because his pictures comprised mostly " Magdalens." The real name of the
French landscape painter, **Claude Lorraine** (born
1600, died 1682), was Claude Gelée *of* Lorraine;
that of Paolo Veronese, or **Paul Veronese** (born
1528, died 1588), was Paolo Cagliari, his birth having
taken place in Verona; and that of Jacopa da
Bassano, called **Il Bassano** (born 1510, died 1592),
was Jacopa da Ponte, whose native place was
Bassano, in the Venetian State. Pietro Vanucci
(born 1446, died 1524), though recognizing Città
della Pieve as his birthplace, was all his life established in the neighbouring city of Perugia, where he
claimed the right of citizenship; hence the origin of
his more common name **Il Perugino.** Francesco
Rossi (born 1510, died 1563), adopted the name of
Del Salviati, in honour of his patron, Cardinal
Salviati, who was his own age exactly, and, strangely
enough, died in the same year as himself. Giuseppe
Ribera (born 1588, died 1656), was popularly surnamed **Lo Spagnoletto** ("the Little Spaniard"), from
the shortness of his stature and his birth at Xativa,
in Spain; while Tommaso Guidi (born 1402, died
1428), merited his better-known name of **Masaccio,**
owing to the slovenliness of his habits, the direct consequence of an all-absorbing attention to his studies.
Jacopo Robusti (born 1512, died 1594) received his
now far more popular name of **Tintoretto** because
his father followed the occupation of a *tintore,* or dyer.
During his lifetime, this celebrated Italian painter
merited the additional sobriquet of **Il Furioso** owing

to the rapidity with which he produced his work. Quintin Matsys (born 1466, died 1530), whose masterpiece, "The Taking Down from the Cross," has achieved a world-wide reputation, is equally known to fame by the name of **The Smith of Antwerp,** owing to the circumstance of having followed for a time, and with great distinction, his father's occupation of a blacksmith. His attachment to the pretty daughter of a painter, however, caused him eventually to forsake the anvil for the palette. Nearer home the historical portrait painter, David Allan (born 1744, died 1796) was surnamed **The Scottish Hogarth** in compliment to his excellence; and William Huggins (born 1821, died 1884), **The Liverpool Landseer,** in favourable comparison with the celebrated English animal painter of that name.

Simon Bolivar, the South American hero (born 1783, died 1830), justly merited the dignified title of **The Liberator;** while General John Charles Fremont (born 1813, died 1890) won the surname of **The Pathfinder** after his fourth successful exploring expedition across the Rocky Mountains in 1842. Lastly, Jonathan Hastings, a farmer of Cambridge, Massachusetts, U.S., was styled **Yankee Jonathan** in consequence of his addiction to the word *Yankee* in the place of "excellent." Thus he would say, "A Yankee good horse," "A Yankee good cider," &c. This individual, however, must not be confounded with "Brother Jonathan," the nickname of the typical American, to which reference is made in another portion of this work.

THE INNS OF COURT.

A S by reference to our article on TAVERN SIGNS it will be seen how the word *Inn* originally denoted a private mansion, it will suffice to state here that the various colleges of the law students in London are styled **Inns** because the chief of them were at one time the residences of the nobility whose family names they still bear. Thus, **Lincoln's Inn** was the town mansion of the Earls of Lincoln, **Gray's Inn,** of the Earls Gray, **Furnival's Inn,** of the Lords Furnival, and **Clifford's Inn,** of the Lords Clifford. The two first-named, together with the Inner and Middle Temple, are the principal **Inns of Court,** so called because the earliest seminaries for the study of the law were established in one of the courts of the King's palace. The Inns of lesser import are :—**Serjeants' Inn,** originally the establishment of the "Frères Serjens," or Serving Brothers to the Knights Templars who occupied **The Temple** close by ; **Barnard's Inn**— sold and abolished in 1881—named after its ancient owner ; **Staple Inn,** formerly the Hall of the Merchants of the Staple, *i.e.,* wool ; **Clement's Inn** and **Dane's Inn,** so designated from their proximity to the Church of St. Clement-Danes; and **New**

Inn, the latest of all the Inns erected in the early part of the last century. **Thavie's Inn** no longer exists, but the title still adheres to a range of modern buildings erected upon its site. No person of the name of Thavie ever owned or occupied the original premises; nevertheless, when the Inn was established as an appendage to Lincoln's Inn, about the middle of the fourteenth century, the Benchers unanimously agreed to perpetuate the memory of one John Thavie, an armourer who, dying in the year 1348, bequeathed a number of houses in Holborn, representing considerable rentals, to the neighbouring church of St. Andrew, and named it " Thavie's Inn " accordingly.

The senior members of the Inns of Court are styled **Benchers** by reason of the benches on which they formerly sat.

RACES.

GOODWOOD RACES are held once a year in Goodwood Park, the property of the Duke of Richmond; **Ascot Races,** on Ascot Heath, in Berkshire, and **Epsom Races,** on Epsom Downs, near London. The **Derby Stakes,** at Epsom, were named after Edward Smith Stanley, twelfth Earl of Derby, who founded them in 1780, the year after he established the **Oaks Stakes;** so called from an inn known as " Lamberts' Oaks," originally erected by the Hunters' Club and rented by a family named Lambert upon land which subsequently passed into the possession of the Derby family. The **St. Leger Stakes,** otherwise the **Doncaster St. Leger,** annually run for at Doncaster, were established by Colonel Anthony St. Leger in 1776.

A **Hurdle Race** is one in which hurdles are placed at different points along the course. A **Steeplechase** is confined to thoroughbred hunters whose riders are bound to make for the winning-post straight across the country, guided by flags displayed on the highest points along the line, and to clear whatever ditches, fences, walls, or other obstacles that may lie in their course. The term originated from the incident of an unsuccessful hunting-party agreeing to race to the village church, of which the steeple was just in sight; and he who touched the building first with his whip was to be declared the winner. A **Scratched Horse** is one whose name has been struck out of the final list of runners in a particular race. A **Sweepstake** is a term used to denote the whole amount staked by different persons upon one race, and cleared literally " at one sweep " by the fortunate individual who has backed the winner.

LONDON CHURCHES AND BUILDINGS.

IN all probability the name of **Westminster Abbey** would never have come into existence had it not been necessary to distinguish the Abbey Church lying to the west of St. Paul's (founded by Ethelbert in 610) from another Abbey Church that stood upon the rising ground now known as Tower Hill. Consequently, the one was described as the *West Minster*, the other the *East Minster;* and when, in course of time, the latter was swept away, the western edifice not only retained the description of " The West Minster," but gave its name also to the district around. The earliest mention of West Minster occurs in a Saxon charter dated 785.

The **Temple** comprised the chief seat in this country of the Knights Templars after their return from the Holy Land. The **Savoy Chapel** is a modern edifice built by the Queen to replace the original, destroyed by fire July, 7, 1864, which formed the only remaining portion of the old **Savoy Palace** erected by Peter of Savoy, the uncle of Eleanor, queen of Henry III., in 1249, on land granted to him by that monarch.

The Church of **St. Clement-Danes** owes its

compound title to the fact of being dedicated to St. Clement, and of Harold, a Danish king, together with several other Danes lying buried within its walls. The Church of **St. Mary-le-Bow,** Cheapside, otherwise **Bow Church,** was so denominated because it was the first church ever built upon bows or arches. The Church of **St. Mary Woolnoth,** at the corner of Lombard Street and King William Street, is supposed to be a corruption of St. Mary Woolnough, so called by way of distinction from a neighbouring church of " St. Mary of the Wool," that stood beside the beam or wool-staple. The Church of **St. Mary-Axe,** now vanished, received this name from its situation opposite to a shop that displayed an axe for its sign. The Church of **St. Catherine Cree,** Leadenhall Street, is properly St. Catherine and Trinity, being originally a chapel dedicated to St. Catherine in the churchyard of the priory church of Holy Trinity, afterwards merged into the parishes of Christ Church, St. Mary Magdalen, and St. Michael. The Church of **St. Catherine Coleman,** Fenchurch Street, dedicated to St. Catherine, is so designated because it was built in a large garden belonging to a person named Coleman. The Church of **St. Margaret Pattens,** Rood Lane, did not receive its denomination from the patten-makers who congregated in this neighbourhood, but because its roof was formerly decorated with gilt spots or *patines;* a patine being the name of a small circular dish of gold used to cover the chalice at the altar. Lovers of Shakespeare may recollect the passage in the *Merchant of Venice* where Lorenzo, referring to the stars, says :—

> " Sit, Jessica : Look how the floor of heaven
> Is thick inlaid with patines of bright gold ;
> There's not the smallest orb which thou behold'st,
> But in his motion like an angel sings,
> Still quiring to the young-ey'd cherubins ;
> Such harmony is in immortal souls,
> But whilst this muddy vesture of decay
> Doth grossly close it in, we cannot hear it."

The original **Church of St. Sepulchre,** founded during the time of the Crusades, was so denominated in honour of the Holy Sepulchre at Jerusalem. The name of **St. Bride's Church,** Fleet Street, is a contraction of St. Bridget's Church. The Church of **St. Andrew Undershaft,** Leadenhall Street, dedicated to St. Andrew, was originally so called because its steeple was of lesser altitude than the tall shaft or maypole which stood opposite the south door. Hence, the church was literally " under the shaft." The parish of St. Mary-Axe is now united to that of St. Andrew Undershaft. The Church of **St. Helen's,** Bishopsgate, was built and dedicated to St. Helena, the mother of Constantine, in 1180, just thirty years before William Fitzwilliam, a rich goldsmith, founded in connection therewith a priory of Benedictine nuns, dedicated to the Holy Cross and St. Helena. The neighbouring Church of **St. Ethelburga** was so named in honour of the daughter of King Ethelbert. The Church of **All-**

hallowes Barking, at the bottom of Mark Lane, derived the second portion of its title from the fact that it belonged to the ancient abbey and convent at Barking, in Essex. **St. Olave's Church,** Tooley Street, is properly described as **St. Olaf's Church,** being dedicated to Olaf, a Norwegian prince of great renown, who came over to this country at the invitation of the King Ethelred, and rendered good service in expelling the Danes.

The central portion of the Tower of London, supposed to have been built by Julius Cæsar, is known as the **White Tower** on account of the white stone employed in its construction. In the **Bloody Tower** the Infant Princes were murdered by order of their uncle, Richard III.; and in the **Beauchamp Tower,** Thomas de Beauchamp, Earl of Warwick, was imprisoned by Richard II. for leading the conspiracy of the Barons for the removal of Sir Simon de Burley, the young King's favourite. At the accession of Henry IV. the Earl obtained his liberty. **Traitors' Gate** denotes the river gate by which all State prisoners convicted of high treason were admitted into the Tower. **Newgate Prison** derived its name from its original situation next to the newest of the five principal gates of the City. The prison is first mentioned in history under date 1207. The present gloomy edifice was built in 1782. The open space between the prison and the Old Bailey was formerly known as the **Press Yard,** because here it was that prisoners who refused to plead upon trial were barbarously pressed to death. The **Old**

Bailey Sessions House received its name from the street in which it stands [*see* OLD BAILEY in the article "LONDON STREETS AND SQUARES."]   The old **Marshalsea Prison,** Southwark, abolished and pulled down in 1842, was so called because it contained the Court of the Knight-Marshal, whose duty it was to settle disputes occurring between the members of the Royal Household.   This office now belongs to the Steward of the Royal Household.   **Bridewell** was a corruption of " St. Bridget's Well," discovered in the grounds attached to an ancient hospital, afterwards converted into a house of correction for females.   An iron pump let into the wall of the churchyard at the upper end of Bride Lane indicates the exact spot where the dames of old were wont to drink the virtuous waters.   The **Fleet Prison** took its name from the river, now a common sewer, near which it stood.   The northern boundary of the prison is now defined by **Fleet Lane,** which runs from Farringdon Street to the Old Bailey.

St. John's Gate, Clerkenwell, is the sole remaining portion of the priory of St. John of Jerusalem, the seat in this country of the Knights Hospitallers, instituted by Godfrey de Boulogne.   The Gate now forms the headquarters of the St. John's Ambulance Association.   **Temple Bar** was not one of the City fortifications, but the ordinary gateway of the Temple. It was popularly known as **The City Golgotha,** owing to the spiked heads of traitors exposed thereon —*Golgotha* being Hebrew for " the place of skulls." The Bar was taken down in 1878.   **London Bridge**

—that is to say, the original structure—was the first bridge over the Thames. The present structure was thrown open August 1, 1831. **Billingsgate** traces its origin to Belin, one of the early kings of Britain, who built a gate on the site of the present market and gave it his name. **St. Katherine's Docks** received their title from an ancient hospital dedicated to St. Katherine, swept away by their construction in the year 1828. **The Mint** is so called in accordance with the Anglo-Saxon *mynet*, coin [*see* MONEY]. The **Trinity House,** the seat of the Trinity Corporation, which controls the pilotage of the Thames and the various lighthouses, buoys, harbour-dues, &c., around our coast, owed its foundation to Sir Thomas Spert, Comptroller of the Navy of Henry VIII., and commander of the *Harry Grace de Dieu*, originally situated at Deptford; it was incorporated in 1529 under the style of " The Master-Wardens and Assistants of the Guild, or Fraternity, or Brotherhood, of the most glorious and undivisible Trinity, and St. Clement, in the parish of Deptford, Stroud, in the County of Kent." The present edifice was built in 1795. **Crosby Hall,** Bishopsgate, at one time a palace, but now converted into a restaurant, was built by Sir John Crosby about the middle of the fifteenth century. The **Congregational Memorial Hall,** Farringdon Road, which occupies part of the site of the old Fleet Prison, was built in 1872 to memorate the ejection of more than two thousand Church of England ministers from their charges, August 24, 1662,

consequent upon their refusal to subscribe to the
" Act of Uniformity " [*see* NONCONFORMISTS].
The **Guildhall** is the hall of the City guilds;
the word GUILD being derived from the Anglo-
Saxon *gildan,* to pay, alluding to the fee paid for
membership. **Doctors' Commons,** originally established as a college for the Professors of Canon
and Civil Law, received its name from the rule
which required the Doctors to dine at a common
table. That sombre-looking structure, the **College
of Arms,** otherwise **Heralds' College,** is the office
where the records of the genealogical descent of all
our noble families are preserved, and where searches
for coats-of-arms may be instituted. The Corporation of the College dates back to the year
1484. The General Post Office is officially denominated **St. Martin's-le-Grand** because it occupies the site of a collegiate church and sanctuary
of that name founded by Within, King of Kent in
750, and chartered by William the Conqueror in
1068.

The **Charterhouse,** originally a monastery of the
Carthusians, is a corruption of *La Chartreuse,* the
name of the district in France where this religious
Order first came into existence. **Christ's Hospital,**
also known as the **Blue Coat School,** from the
colour of the coats worn by the boys, retains the
ancient designation of a church and school belonging
to the Grey Friars. It is only in modern times, by
the way, that the term **Hospital** has come to be exclusively applied in this country to a refuge for the

sick. Properly understood, a hospital denotes a house intended for the reception and accommodation of travellers ; the source of the word being the Latin *hospitalis,* pertaining to a guest, based upon *hospes,* a stranger, a guest, and from which we derive the word HOSPITALITY. The great Bernardine monastery on the summit of the Alps, devoted to the good work of rescuing snow-bound travellers, is appropriately denominated a **Hospice,** which answers to our Hospital. **St. Bartholomew's Hospital** was founded by Rahare, a monk attached to the neighbouring Priory of St. Bartholomew in 1123 ; whereas **Guy's Hospital** arose out of the bequest of £238,292, by the will of Thomas Guy, a benevolent bookseller of Lombard Street, who died in 1722. **Bedlam** is a contraction of **Bethlehem Hospital,** a lazar-house named after the Hospital of St. Mary at Bethlehem, and converted into a lunatic asylum in 1815. This was the common designation in ancient times for a refuge for the poor, the word **Bethlehem** expressing the Hebrew for " a house of bread " ; but in more modern times the synonym **Lazar-house** was substituted in allusion to Lazarus, who picked up the crumbs under the table of Dives. A refuge for fallen women has always borne the name of a **Magdalen Hospital** in honour of Mary Magdalen.

St. James's Palace marks the site of an ancient leper hospital dedicated to St. James the Less, Bishop of Jerusalem. The present edifice was built by Henry VIII. in 1530. **Buckingham Palace** displaced old Buckingham House, the town mansion

of John Sheffield, Duke of Buckingham, in the year
1825. The total cost to the nation of this "desirable
residence" was £1,000,000. **Marlborough House**
was originally the town residence of John, Duke of
Marlborough, erected by Sir Christopher Wren in
1709. **Somerset House** reverted to the Crown by
the attainder of its owner, Edward Seymour, Duke
of Somerset, the Lord Protector of Edward VI.,
executed January 22, 1552. **Whitehall** received
its name from the fresh appearance of its exterior as
contrasted with the ancient buildings on the opposite
side of the way. The present fabric, viz., **The
Banquetting Hall,** is merely a vestige of the
palace originally set apart by Cardinal Wolsey for
the London See of York : whence he gave it the name
of "York House." The **Horse Guards** is so called
because a troop of Horse Guards are regularly
quartered here. **Dover House** was named after its
owner, the Hon. George Agar Ellis, afterwards
created Lord Dover ; and **York House,** after the
Duke of York and Albany who bought it in 1789.
Devonshire House, Piccadilly, is the town residence
of the Duke of Devonshire. **Apsley House,** Hyde
Park Corner, well known as the residence of the Duke
of Wellington, received its name from Henry Apsley,
Lord Chancellor, afterwards created Lord Bathurst,
who built it in 1784. **Chandos House,** Cavendish
Square, was the residence of James Brydges, "the
Princely Duke of Chandos." The **Albany,** Picca-
dilly, perpetuates the memory of the Duke of York
and Albany, who acquired it from Lord Melbourne

in exchange for his older residence, York House, in Whitehall. **Burlington House,** the home of the Royal Academy of Arts and quite a number of learned societies, was built by Sir John Denham, the poet and judge, in 1718, and refronted by the celebrated amateur architect, Richard Boyle, Earl of Burlington and Cork, in 1731. This palatial edifice was purchased by the State in 1854. The **Soane Museum,** Lincoln's Inn Fields, was the private collection of Sir John Soane, the architect and antiquary, who died in 1837. **The Rolls Chapel,** Chancery Lane, bears this name because it was annexed by patent to the office of the Master of the Rolls of Chancery after the banishment of the Jews from England in the year 1290. The history of the chapel dates from 1283, when Henry III. founded it for the reception of the Jewish rabbis converted to Christianity.

The **Painted Hall,** Greenwich Hospital, owes its name to its magnificently decorated ceiling. **Vanburgh Castle,** Blackheath, was built in the castellated style by Sir John Vanburgh, in 1717. **Rye House,** famous for being the scene of the conspiracy to assassinate Charles II., which was discovered June 12, 1683, is so called from the rye on which it stands; RYE being an Old English term for a common, derived from *ree*, a watercourse: hence PECKHAM RYE.

Bruce Castle, Tottenham, has a history all its own. The present structure dates back to the latter part of the seventeenth century; but the original building was erected by Earl **Waltheof,** whose marriage with Judith, the niece of William the Conqueror, brought him portions of the earldoms of Northumberland and Huntingdon.   Their only daughter, Maud, on becoming the wife of David I., King of Scotland, placed him in possession of the Huntingdon estates, and, as appended to that property, the manor of Tottenham, in Middlesex. Ultimately these possessions descended to Robert Bruce, the brother of William III., King of Scotland.   The contention between Robert Bruce and John Baliol for the Scottish throne being decided in favour of the latter, the former retired to England, and settling on his grandfather's estate at Tottenham, repaired the castle to which he gave the name of " The Castle Bruce." **Lincoln House,** Enfield, was the residence of the second and third Earls of Lincoln in the seventeenth century. **Sandford House,** Stoke Newington, is interesting as having been the residence of Thomas Day, the author of " Sandford and Merton " (born 1748, died 1789). **Cromwell House,** Highgate, now a Convalescent Hospital for sick children, was occupied for some time by Oliver Cromwell, who built **Ireton House,** close by, for Henry Ireton, his son-in-law, in 1630 ; while **Lauderdale House,** lately a Convalescent Home in connection with St. Bartholomew's Hospital, was the residence of the Earls of Lauderdale during the seventeenth century. WATERLOW PARK, in this neighbourhood—in fact, comprising among other valuable property the grounds appertaining to Lauderdale House—was generously presented to the London public by Sir Sydney Waterlow, in November, 1890. The **Clock House,** Hampstead, originally displayed a clock in place of the present sun-dial. **Rosslyn House,** Hampstead, which gives the name to ROSSLYN HILL PARK, was erected by Alexander Wedderburn, first Earl of Rosslyn and Lord Chancellor of England, in 1795. **Erskine House,** Hampstead, adjoining " The Spaniards," was the residence of Lord Erskine, Lord Chancellor of England, who died here in 1823.

Strawberry Hill, the celebrated palace of curiosities built by Horace Walpole in 1750, received its name from the rising ground upon which it stood. The building was sold by public auction, and purchased by Baron H. de Stein, in July, 1883. **Orleans House,** Twickenham, now a club, was named after Louis Philippe of France, who resided in it when he was simply Duc d'Orleans. **Essex House,** Putney, was one of the many residences of Robert Devereaux, Earl of Essex, the favourite of Queen Elizabeth. **Bristol House,** Putney, was, until recently, the property of the Bristol family. **Craven Cottage,** Fulham, was built by the Countess of Craven, afterwards created Margravine of Anspach. **Munster House,** Fulham, derived its title from its one-time resident, Melesina Schulenberg, created Duchess of Munster in 1716. **Peterborough House,** Parson's Green, was formerly the mansion of the Mordaunts, Earls of Peterborough. **Sussex**

House, Hammersmith, was the favourite residence of the late Duke of Sussex. **Holland House,** Kensington, owes its name to Henry Rich, Earl of Holland, by whose father-in-law, Sir William Cope, it was built in 1607. Here Charles James Fox, the eminent orator and statesman (born 1749, died 1806), passed many of his earlier years ; here also Joseph Addison, the poet and essayist, died in the year 1719.

The **Albert Hall, Albert Memorial, Albert Bridge,** and **Albert Palace,** each preserve the memory of the Prince Consort, whose death took place in 1861. The **Crystal Palace,** opened by the Queen, June 10, 1854, derived its title from its glass structure, which, when the sun shines upon it, glistens like crystal. The **Alexandra Palace** was named after the Princess of Wales, who was to have opened the original building, May 24, 1873 ; but, for some unexplained reason, she did not perform that ceremony. **Olympia,** opened December, 1886, is an appropriate designation for a huge edifice eminently adapted for every variety of popular amusement. The allusion is to Olympia, in Greece, where the celebrated "Olympian Games" were anciently held every fourth year. The **Polytechnic Institution,** Regent Street (now the Y. M. C. A.), was designated in strict conformity with its set purpose as an educational establishment, viz., from the two Greek words *polus*, many, and *techne*, an art. **St. George's Hall** was originally, when opened in 1867, St. George's Opera House, so styled because situated in the fashionable parish of St. George's,

Hanover Square. The **Egyptian Hall,** built in 1812, is a particularly well-chosen title; at least, it appears so at the present day, since the regular performances of those modern magicians, Messrs. Maskelyne and Cooke, have long ago become one of the institutions, if not actually one of the sights, of the Metropolis. **St. James's Hall** was named after the parish church just opposite. **Willis's Rooms,** so called after their late proprietor, were originally opened by a Scotsman named Almack, under the style of **Almack's Assembly Rooms,** February 12, 1765. **Exeter Hall** was built in the year 1830 in the grounds of Exeter House, which also gave the name to **Exeter 'Change,** erected in 1680 and pulled down in 1829 [*see* EXETER STREET]. The world-famous waxworks exhibition known as **Madame Tussaud's** retains the name of its foundress (born 1760, died 1850) who first set up her figures at the old Lyceum Theatre in 1802, and after undergoing a variety of misfortunes settled down permanently in Baker Street in the year 1833.

Scotland Yard, the headquarters of the Metropolitan Police, received its name from an ancient palace erected on this spot for the accommodation of the Scottish kings in the days when they were annually required to pay homage to the Crown of England at Westminster. The first monarch so accommodated was Kenneth II. (died 854); the last was Margaret, Queen of Scots, the sister of Henry VIII. **Lord's Cricket Ground,** familiarly styled

Lord's, owes its existence to Thomas Lord, who established, upon land of his own, first on the site of Dorset Square in 1780, and subsequently on its present site, the only cricketing ground where genteel players could meet to enjoy this game without fear of rubbing shoulders with the City apprentices. Previous to his enterprise the formation of a private Cricket Club had never been thought of.

Tattersall's, the well-known rendezvous for the sale of horses, was opened by Richard Tattersall near Hyde Park Corner in 1766, and removed to Knightsbridge April 10, 1865.

Lloyd's Rooms, better known as **Lloyd's,** derived this title from Edward Lloyd, a coffee-house keeper in Abchurch Lane, whose premises became the regular resort of merchants and others interested in shipping. The original location of a special office for the transaction of mercantile business over the Royal Exchange took place in 1775 ; but the name of the genial coffee-house keeper was by common consent transferred with it. On the destruction by fire of the first Royal Exchange, in 1838, " Lloyd's " was temporarily removed until the completion of the present building in 1844.

The entrance to the privileged precincts of the Stock Exchange is called **Capel Court,** because it marks the residence of Sir William Capel, Lord Mayor of London in the year 1504. The term **Exchange** owes its origin to the French *echanger*, to trade, to barter. The object of the original **Royal Exchange,** founded by Sir Thomas Gresham in

1506 and opened by Queen Elizabeth amid sundry
public rejoicings over the event (which accounts for
the prenomen " Royal "), January 31, 1571, was to
provide a convenient place where the merchants,
bankers, and brokers of the City could meet throughout the day for the transaction of business. The
Stock Exchange is the great money mart of the
world [*see* STOCK in the article " MONEY "].

The **Bankers' Clearing House,** in Lombard
Street, is the establishment where all cheques,
drafts, and bills drawn upon the various bankers
are sorted, distributed, and balanced up. The
Railway Clearing House, adjoining Euston
Railway Station, is a similar establishment devoted
to the adjustment of the value represented by the
tickets issued by the different Railway Companies.
In conclusion, the title of **Mansion House,** though
somewhat suggestive of tautology, may be accepted
as denoting *the* house of all other houses, since it is
the official residence of the Lord Mayor.

CLASS NAMES AND NICKNAMES.

AN unmarried female originally received the designation of **Spinster** from her employment at the distaff or spindle. According to the practical notions of our Anglo-Saxon forefathers, a female was not considered fit to enter the married state until she had made for herself a complete set of body, bed, and table-linen. Hence the significance of the term **Wife,** derived from the Anglo-Saxon *wif*, by virtue of the verb *wyfan*, to weave. The designation **Widow** is an Indo-European importation, derived from the Sanskrit *vid-hava*, without husband. **Grass Widow,** denoting a woman temporarily separated from her husband, is a corruption of " Grace Widow " —in other words, a widow by grace, or courtesy. The word **Chaperon** is French, derived from the chapeau, or cap, worn by the duennas of Spain. **Duenna,** signifying a guardian, is Spanish, founded upon the Latin *domina*, a mistress. The title of **Dowager,** which distinguishes a widow left with a jointure from the wife of her late husband's heir, comes from the French *douairière*, built upon the verb *douaire*, to dower. The name of **Blue Stocking** arose from the colour of the stockings worn by the members of the lady clubs in England during the days of Boswell. Gentlemen were not excluded from these assemblies, but the wearing of blue stockings was a *sine quâ non* of admittance. The last surviving member of the original BLUE STOCKING CLUB, founded by Mrs. Montague in 1780, died in 1840. The earliest Blue Stocking assembly came into existence at Venice, under the title of *Della Calza* in the year 1400. A lady's-maid is familiarly styled an **Abigail,** in allusion to the handmaid who introduced herself to David (1 *Samuel* xxv. 23). This class-name came into particular prominence during the early part of the eighteenth century, in compliment to Abigail Hill, the maiden name of Mrs. Mashem, the waiting-woman of Queen Anne. A Parisian shop or work-girl is known as a **Grisette** on account of the grey cloth of which her dress is made. In olden times all inferior classes in France were expected to be clad in *gris, i.e.,* grey. **Colleen** is the native Irish for girl ; and **Colleen Bawn** for a blonde girl. How little the latter expression is understood by actresses is shown by the way in which some of them essay to impersonate (?) the heroine of Dion Boucicault's well-known drama whilst wearing their own dark hair or a dark wig. Truly, a little knowledge is a useful thing !

As nowadays comprehended, a **Milliner** is one who retails hats, feathers, bonnets, ribbons, and similar appurtenances to female costume. The name is really a corruption of *Milaner,* alluding to the city of Milan, which at one time set the fashion to the north of Europe in all matters of taste and elegance. **Haberdasher** is a modern form of the Old English word *Hapertaser,* or a retailer of hapertas cloth, the width of which was settled by Magna Charta. **Grocer** is a contraction and modified spelling of **Engrosser,** the denomination of a tradesman who, in the Middle Ages, claimed a monopoly for the supply of provisions. A vendor of vegetables is appropriately called a **Greengrocer.** An innkeeper is facetiously styled a **Boniface** in honour of a devout and hospitable man whom St. Augustine caused to be canonized, and who subsequently became the patron saint of Germany. Shakespeare, Dante, Bacon, and Lamb never tired of referring to Boniface. **Ostler** is a corruption of the French *hostelier,* an innkeeper; hence we sometimes speak of an inn as a HOSTELRY. The term **Carpenter,** from the Latin *carpentum,* a waggon, originally denoted a mechanic who constructed the wooden body of a vehicle of any kind, as distinguished from the **Wheelwright;** but in process of time the same term came to be applied to artificers in timber generally. The provincial name for such a one is a **Joiner,** literally a joiner of wooden building materials. In some districts of England a shoemaker still bears the name of **Cordwainer.** Formerly all shoemakers were styled Cordwainers, because they were workers in CORDWAIN, a corruption of CORDOVAN, which was the name of a

particular kind of leather brought from Cordova.
The designation **Tailor** is an Anglicized form of
the French *Tailleur*, derived from the verb *tailler*,
to cut. [For **Tallyman** *see* TALLY, in the article
" MONEY."] A Pawnbroker is familiarly called
Uncle, in perpetuation of an ancient pun on the
Latin word *uncus*, a hook. For, whereas in modern
times the spout is employed as a means of communication between the pawnshop and the store-rooms
overhead, the Roman pawnbrokers used a large
hook ; and accordingly, the expression " Gone to
the *uncus*," was equivalent to our slang phrase " Up
the spout." A **Barber** derives his class-title from
the Latin *barba*, a beard. Rude and semi-civilized
tribes were anciently called **Barbarians,** because
they belonged to no order of society. Between the
fourteenth and sixteenth centuries the hairdressers
of this country combined the practice of surgery,
and were accordingly styled **Barber-Surgeons.**
The surviving " Barber's Pole " attests this fact.
The separation of the two professions took place
in 1540.

A shepherd or an ideal farmer bears the poetical
description of an **Arcadian,** in allusion to the
Arcadians, who were a pastoral people. A friendly
adviser is designated a **Mentor,** in memory of the
wise and faithful counsellor of Telemachus so named.
The word **Usher** signifies a doorkeeper, agreeably
to the Old French *huisher*, a door. **Bachelor** comes
from the Welsh *bach*, small, young. This name
originally meant one inexperienced in anything.

The title of **Bachelor of Arts** denotes a degree next below that of **Master of Arts.**

Beefeaters is a vulgar perversion of *Buffetiers*, as the Yeoman of the Guard were styled during the reign of Henry VIII., on account of their attendance upon the King's *Buffet*, or side-table. The word BUFFET is French, derived from the Spanish *búfia*, a wineskin. The civic guardians of law and order are denominated **Police** in accordance with the Greek *polis*, the city. For many years after the establishment of the Police through the measures of Sir Robert Peel (in Ireland, as the national constabulary in 1814; in London as a regular force in 1829), all **Policemen** were nicknamed **Bobbies** and **Peelers,** in allusion to their founder. **Bow Street Runners** were the original London detective force; so called because their headquarters was Bow Street, whence they were despatched to any part of the country in quest of the perpetrator of a particular crime. The predecessors of the Police were a set of decrepit old watchmen whose regular habit was to fall asleep in their boxes with their lanthorns beside them. These were derisively nicknamed **Old Charlies;** while their natural enemies, who loved nothing so much as to turn their boxes upon them, to molest defenceless females, mutilate males, and in many other ways to terrorize the peaceable inhabitants of the Metropolis, styled themselves first of all **Scourers,** and at a later date **Mohocks,** after the North American Indian tribe of that name. During the years 1859 and 1860 an even more grievous terror haunted the

streets of London in the persons of **The Garrotters,**
so called from the *Garrotte*, the instrument with
which condemned malefactors are strangled in Spain.
The punishment of the " cat o' nine tails " for
" Garrotting," which came into operation July 13,
1861, gradually put an end to the practice. The
latest terror of the streets which, unhappily, abounds
in American cities, are the **Sandbaggers,** so called
because they stun their victims with an ordinary
sand-bag, such as is used to keep the draught from
penetrating between a pair of window-sashes ; after
which robbery becomes an easy matter.

Pleasanter it is to turn from the birds of night to
the fops and dandies by day. The word **Fop** comes
from the German *foppen*, to make a fool of ; and
Dandy from the French *dandin*, a ninny. Between
these two poor specimens of humanity there is no
perceptible difference. The **Macaronies** of the last
century derived their designation from the fashionable
" Macaroni Clubs " to which they belonged. The
modern class-title of **Masher** finds its origin in the
Romany or gipsy word *mâsha*, signifying " to fasci-
nate the eye." *En passant*, the term **Gipsy** is a
corruption of *Egyptian*, so called because the
original family or tribe of low caste Hindoos expelled by Timour about the year 1399 eventually
travelled into Europe by way of Egypt. The **Gipsies**
were also in former times known as **Bohemians,**
from the district in which they first attracted popular
attention before they scattered themselves over
Western Europe. Hence, any individual whose

habits are unconventual, and to a certain extent
nomadic, is styled a **Bohemian.** The name of
The Upper Ten applied to the aristocracy, is
short for " The Upper Ten Thousand," a term originally applied by N. P. Willis, the American poet
(born 1807, died 1867), to the fashionables of New
York who, at the time he introduced it, numbered
about ten thousand. A distinctly latter-day expression conveying much the same signification is **The
Four Hundred,** by which we are left to conclude
that the " select " society of New York must have
undergone a considerable weeding-out during the
last twenty years.

The temperance terms **Teetotal** and **Teetotaler**
originated in the stuttering exhortation of one
Richard Turner, an artizan of Preston, who, while
addressing a meeting of abstainers in September,
1833, observed that " Nothing but t-t-total absti-
nence will do ! " Several bodies of total abstainers
from alcoholic beverages in England and America
style themselves **Rechabites,** after the descendants
of Jonadab, the son of Rechab, who lived in tents and
foreswore wine. Others rejoice in the name of
Good Templars, after the Templars of old. The
Good Templar Movement cannot be accurately
described as a *crusade* against drink ; but the
League of the Cross, established by the Roman
Catholics for the total suppression of drunkenness,
is, in title and in fact, one of the most powerful
crusades ever distinguished in modern times.

A sailor is called a **Jack Tar** because he puts on

tarpaulin " overalls " in " dirty weather." **Long-shoreman** is a corruption of *alongshoreman, i.e.,* a wharfinger, &c. **Navvy** is a contraction of *Navigator,* which name was first given to the labourers employed in the construction of canals for inland navigation. A cabman is popularly styled a **Jehu** in allusion to one of the kings of Israel noted for his furious driving. A **Jerry Builder** is so called after one Jeremiah, a London builder who amassed a fortune by putting up houses with inferior materials in order to sell them at a large profit. A **Journeyman** is properly one who hires himself out to work by the day, agreeably to the first portion of the word *Jour,* the French for day. A debt-collector is known as a **Dun,** and his persistence is styled " Dunning," in memory of Joe Dun, a famous bailiff of Lincoln, who was so successful in the discharge of his duties that it became quite customary when an individual refused to pay his debts to exclaim, " Why don't you *Dun* him for it ? " which was tantamount to saying, " Why don't you send *Dun* to arrest him ? " Whilst on the subject of law, we may here add that the expression **A Man of Straw,** employed to denote a person without capital or means, originated in the days when a certain class of men, chiefly ruined tradesmen, found it a profitable occupation to hire themselves out as witnesses in the law courts. The recognized mark of these persons was a wisp of straw protruding from their shoes ; and as often as a lawyer stood in need of a convenient witness to prove his case, he knew by the presence of " a pair of straw shoes " in court that the owner of the said shoes would recollect and swear to any incident in consideration of a fee.

Costermonger is a corruption of *Costardmonger,* a seller of the famous costard apple introduced into this country by the Dutch in 1736. Both these terms are used by Shakespeare ; nevertheless, they bore a totally different signification in his time. The word **Monger** comes from the Anglo-Saxon *mongere,* one who trades. An itinerant salesman in the olden time was styled a **Pedlar,** in accordance with the Latin *pedes,* the feet, because he travelled on foot ; whereas **Hawker** comes from the German *hoken,* to carry on the back, to retail. Hawkers and Pedlars were first licensed in England in 1698. An itinerant salesman of another kind is known as a **Cheap Jack** on account of the word " cheap " which is Saxon for market, derived from *ceapan,* to buy. A travelling medicine-vendor originally received the nickname of **Quack-doctor,** or **Quack,** from *Quacksalber,* the German term for quicksilver, because, differing from the regular practitioners, he resorted to mercury and other dangerous ingredients. At times a Quack, or any other individual gifted with humorous colloquial powers, is dubbed a **Merry Andrew,** in allusion to Andrew Borde, a physician of the time of Henry VIII., noted for his facetious manners and sayings. **Juggler** is a corruption of *jongleur,* the French designation of one of the companions of the troubadours, whose business it was to supplement the lyrical accomplishments of the latter with feats of sleight-of-hand and other tricks 'for the amusement of the company. **A Stump Orator** is properly one who delivers a speech from the stump of a tree ; the literal meaning of a STUMP SPEECH being thus explained.

The now approbrious name of **Blackguard** was formerly given to the scullions or dirty dependants of the English Court who washed out the saucepans, carried coals up to the kitchens, and performed other menial duties. As the " Guards of Honour" in the Royal Household were distinguished by their fine appearance, so these kitchen-men were equally distinguished by their grimy appearance ; consequently the latter were styled " Black Guards." The origin of the word **Scullion** was the Norman-French *esculle*, a porringer or dish. The place where the dishes are cleansed is still called a SCULLERY, while the domestic who performs such work bears the name of **Scullery Maid.** A rascal or sharper is designated a **Blackleg,** because such a one was generally to be found among the lower orders of turf and sporting men at the time these were especially characterized by the wearing of black top-boots. A **Plunger** is one who bets heavily either on the turf or at the gaming-table, without consideration for the risks he incurs. A **Bookmaker** is so called because he arranges his book, *i.e.*, his bets, in such a manner that his losses and gains upon each day's racing must balance themselves. The Book-maker who absconds after a race in order to avoid paying those who have entered bets with him and

won is styled a **Welsher,** in allusion to the thieving
propensities of a certain race of people, as set forth
in the old song, which begins, " Taffy was a Welsh-
man, Taffy was a thief," &c.   The word **Burglar**
is made up of the Old English *burgh,* a borough,
derived from the German *burg,* a fortified place, and
the French *lair,* a thief; the allusion being that such
a one breaks into a private dwelling for purposes of
theft.   Down to a comparatively recent date the
common hangman in this country bore the nickname of **Jack Ketch,** really a corruption of Richard
Jacquett, to whom the manor of Tyburn, where our
malefactors were executed prior to the year 1783,
belonged.

A native of London is popularly styled a
Cockney, pursuant to the Old English *cockeney,*
an effeminate person, or rather one who has been
rendered effeminate by the luxuries of the table;
this term tracing its origin directly from the Latin
verb *coquere,* to cook, whence we have the Italian
cuchina, the French *euisine,* the German *küche,* and
the English *kitchen.*   A popular satiric poem of
the thirteenth century, entitled " The Land of
Cockaygne,"—*i.e.,* Kitchen Land, draws a picture
of an imaginary Fool's Paradise, where there is
nothing but eating and drinking, where care, trouble,
and toil find no place—a desirable country for those
monks of the Church who delight in the pleasures
of the table rather than the observance of their
spiritual exercises.   After this performance the term
Cockaigne or **Cockaygne** gradually came to be

applied to our capital city, where *cockenies*, or kitchen-servants, abounded, and where the luxury of good living was supposed to attain its highest development.

A raw youth, or a countryman new to the ways of the world, is dubbed a **Greenhorn**, in reference to the undeveloped horns of a young ox; the word "Green" being derived from the Anglo-Saxon *grêne*, that which is in process of growing. **Nincompoop** is a corruption of the Latin phrase *non compos* [*mentis*], not in sound mind. A person of defective mind is called a **Lunatic**, from the Latin *luna*, the moon, in accordance with the Roman idea that the mind was affected by the changes of the moon. A person addicted to making foolish mistakes is styled a **Dutchman**, in allusion to the dull comprehensions supposed to be possessed by the inhabitants of the Low Countries. The term first came into use as an epithet of derision during the wars with Holland. A **Humbug** is one whose representations, though sounding plausible enough, are not to be relied upon. The origin of this word is as follows: In olden times there resided in the neighbourhood of the Mearns, in Scotland, a gentleman of landed property whose name was Hume, and whose estate was known as " The Bogue." Owing to the great falsehoods which this " Hume of the Bogne " was in the habit of relating about himself, his family, and everything connected with his affairs, it became customary, as often as the people of that district heard anything at all remarkable or absurd to ex-claim, " That is a Hume of the Bogue." The word spelt in its present form first appeared on the title-page of " The Universal Jester : a choice collection of *bonmots* and *humbugs*," published by Fernando Killigrew about the year 1736.   The assurance that Humbug is of such old date can scarcely tend to our satisfaction.

MALT LIQUORS.

AT the present day the terms **Ale** and **Beer** are used somewhat confusedly. The former, derived from the Gaelic and Irish *ól*, drink, is the real name of our national beverage, which, to judge from its intoxicating effects, must, in the days of our forefathers, have been a very strong drink indeed. The latter, on the other hand, is essentially a Saxon word, from the same root as *barm*, signifying "fermented drink," and used to denominate the lighter kinds of fermented liquors generally, as well as other drinks obtained from the roots or leaves of plants, such as GINGER-BEER, SPRUCE-BEER, &c. We still speak of **Old Ales**; whereas **Small Beer** indicates a liquor of very poor quality.

In former times the only varieties of malt liquor in this country were **Ale** and **Beer,** the one strong, the other comparatively weak. To these a third, popularly described as **Twopenny,** was eventually added. However, it was rare that any one of these three was demanded singly; it being the custom, particularly in London, for the working-classes to call either for **Half-and-Half** or **Three Thirds,** meaning a tankard filled with equal portions of ale and beer, or of ale, beer, and twopenny. This custom remained in vogue until the year 1730, when it occurred to Mr. Harwood, a brewer of East London, to prepare a liquor analogous to the mixture of ale, beer, and twopenny; and thus save the time of the tavern-keepers, who were compelled to serve each customer from three different casks. Almost immediately, therefore, he introduced the malt liquor known as **Entire,** because it was drawn *entire* from one cask. It was first retailed at the sign of "The Blue Last," in Curtain Road, Shoreditch, where it soon came to be in active demand by the City porters, who made this house their regular resort, whereupon the enterprising publican adroitly called it **Porter.** The word "Entire" still appears upon the facia-boards of numerous taverns throughout the Metropolis; but who thinks of calling for *Entire* at the present day? By the term **Stout** is implied a malt liquor of the stoutest quality, *i.e.*, having the most body in it.

Stingo expresses an old beer of particular sharpness, in allusion to its *stinging* properties; while **Yorkshire Stingo** is, of course, peculiar to the county of York. Originally the single X displayed on beer-barrels denoted that the liquor had paid a ten shillings' duty. The additional X's are merely brewers' trade-marks, indicating various degrees of strength over and above that of the single X ale.

Concerning German beers, we need only allude to **Mum,** or **Mumm,** which is peculiar to Brunswick, and named after Christoph Mumme, who first

brewed it in 1492 ; **Lager-Bier,** so called because it
is kept in a lager or cellar ; and **Bock-bier,** a liquor
which causes the inconsiderate tippler to caper about
like a *bock*, or goat.

DIAMONDS AND PRECIOUS STONES.

THE word **Diamond** is a corruption of, and synonymous with, **Adamant,** derived from the Greek *adamas,* untamable, infrangible, not to be subdued, in accordance with the prefix *a,* without, and *damas,* to tame, to subdue. As every one must be aware, the diamond is capable of resisting fire.

The great diamonds of the world are the following:— The **Kohinoor,** or " Mountain of Light," weighing 106 carats, came into the possession of Queen Victoria on the annexation of the Punjaub in 1849; the **Mattan** (367 carats) belongs to the Rajah of Mattan ; the **Orloff** (194 carats) preserves the family name of Catherine II. of Russia, who purchased it in 1775; the **Shah** (86 carats), presented by Chosroes I., Shah of Persia, who died in the year 579, to the Czar of Russia ; the **Star of the South** (254 carats), discovered in Brazil by a poor negress in 1853 ; the **Sauci** (106 carats), originally the property of a French gentleman of this name, and bought by the Russian Czar for half a million roubles in 1835 ; the **Regent,** also known as the **Pitt** (137 carats), first acquired by Mr. Pitt, the grandfather of the Earl of Chatham, and subsequently sold to the Duc d'Orleans, Regent of France, for £135,000; the **Pigott** (82¼ carats), brought from India by Lord Pigott sometime previous to 1818, when it came into the possession of Messrs. Rundell and Bridge; the **Dudley** (44½ carats), found at the Cape by a black shepherd in 1868, and, after various changes of ownership, bought by the Earl of Dudley for £30,000; and the **Twin Diamonds,** both found in the bed of the river Vaal at the Cape in 1872.

With regard to precious stones:—the **Turquois** derived its name from Turkey, where it was first found; the **Topaz,** from Topazos, an island in the Red Sea; and the **Agate,** from the Greek *Achates*, a river in Sicily, in the bed of which it was anciently discovered. The term **Amethyst** comes from the Greek *amethustos,* a precious stone, and **Opal,** through the Latin *opalus,* from the Sanskrit *opula,* a precious stone. **Emerald** traces its origin through the French *emerande* to the Latin and Greek *omaragdus;* **Garnet,** through the French *grenat,* from the Latin *granatus;* and **Ruby,** from the Latin *ruber,* red. **Pearl** is an Anglo-Saxon word derived from the Latin *pirula,* a diminutive of pear.

We may conveniently add that the weight of precious stones, as well as that of gold, is regulated by **Carats,** because formerly carat seeds, or the seed of the Abyssinian coral flower were employed for this purpose.

NAVAL AND MILITARY SOBRIQUETS.

THE Roman Manlius (appointed Consul in the year 224 B.C.) received the name of **Torquatus** from the incident of having torn the golden torque or collar from the neck of his adversary in the field. Charles, the son of Pepin d'Heristal, was surnamed **Martel** in recognition of his victory over the Saracens, who attempted the invasion of France in the year 732. According to the chronicler, "he knocked down the foe and crushed them between his axe, as a martel or hammer crushes what it strikes." Robert, Duke of Normandy, the father of William the Conqueror (died 1035), bore the name of **Robert le Diable,** or **Robert the Devil,** on account of his courageous cruelty in war. The Scottish outlaw, Sir William Wallace (born 1270, beheaded 1305), was styled **The Hammer and Scourge of England** by reason of his patriotism. William Douglas, Lord of Nithsdale (died 1390), was known as **Black Douglas** because his frame was tall, strong, and well-built, while his hair was dark and his complexion swarthy. Archibald Douglas, Earl of Angus (died 1514), merited the sobriquet of **Bell**

the Cat for having put to death the upstart favourites of James III., and so prevented the creation of nobles out of architects and masons whom the king particularly patronized. At a meeting convened in the Church of Lauder by the Scottish nobles for the purpose of taking measures to obtain the removal of these persons, Lord Gray had put the question, " But who will bell the cat ? "   " That will I ! " answered Douglas on the instant; and he kept his word, for in the very presence of the king he slew the obnoxious minions with his own hand.

Richard Nevil, Earl of Warwick (born 1420, died 1471), was surnamed **The King Maker** for the reason that while he espoused the cause of the Yorkists, Edward IV. succeeded in his efforts to gain the English Crown; and when, subsequently, he transferred his influence to the Lancastrians, Henry VI. was restored and the usurper deposed.   Harry Percy (born 1364, died 1403) was styled **Hotspur,** and Prince Rupert (born 1619, died 1682) **The Mad Cavalier** because they found it impossible to restrain their rash courage in time of war.   The soldiers of Cromwell, after the Battle of Marston Moor, received the popular name of **Ironsides** on account of their armour and their iron resolution. The sobriquet of **The Almighty Nose** was bestowed upon Oliver Cromwell (born 1599, died 1658), in allusion to his nasal enormity.   Strange, indeed, that he who had attained to the highest position in the land by the sheer force of arms should have been so continually taunted with the length and colour of

his nose! Yet so it was. Nevertheless, there have
been others whose peace of mind was daily threatened
by popular malice in this selfsame respect. Even
the great Roman poet Ovid suffered a lifelong
martyrdom, and became the recipient of the sobriquet
of **Naso,** owing to the possession of an unusually
large nose; just as in modern times Wilson, the
painter, and Cervetto, the violincellist of Drury Lane
Theatre, never succeeded in putting their heads out
of their own doors without being greeted with shouts
of **" Nosey! "** from the mob.

The Duke of Cumberland (born 1721, died 1765)
rightly deserved the opprobrious surname of **The
Bloody Butcher** on account of his merciless
slaughter of the vanquished adherents of the Young
Pretender after the Battle of Culloden. The soldiers
of the Duke of Marlborough (born 1650, died 1722)
familiarly styled their leader **Corporal John** because
he had risen from the rank of Corporal; while
General Bonaparte, afterwards Emperor of the
French (born 1769, died 1821), bore the name of
The Little Corporal, in allusion to his original
rank, his low stature, youthful appearance, and
extraordinary courage. As most readers are aware,
Wellington (born 1769, died 1852) earned the name
of **The Iron Duke** by his iron will and resolution;
and Blucher (born 1742, died 1819) that of **Marshal
Forward,** by his dash and readiness to attack the
enemy in the campaign which terminated in the
Battle of Waterloo. Prince Bismarck, the late
Chancellor of the German Empire (born 1815) owed

his surname of **The Iron Chancellor** to his extra-
ordinary vigour and indomitable will. Helmuth,
Count von Moltke, Field-Marshal of the German
armies (born 1800, died 1891), was popularly surnamed
Helmuth the Taciturn, because though a master
of half a dozen languages, he was never known to
betray himself in one of them. The sobriquet
of **Stonewall Jackson,** possessed by Thomas
Jonathan Jackson, the Confederate General in the
American War of 1861 to 1865, originated with
General Lee, who, after rallying his troops at the
Battle of Bull Run, exclaimed, " There is Jackson,
standing like a stone wall ! " A less complimentary
sobriquet bestowed upon General Andrew Jackson,
President of the United States (born 1767, died
1845), by his own soldiers, was that of **Old
Hickory,** in allusion to his tough, unyielding disposition. The circumstance is thus commented
upon by Parton, the author of Jackson's *Life* :—
" The name of *Old Hickory* was not an instantaneous
inspiration, but a growth. First of all, the remark
was made by some soldier, who was struck with his
commander's pedestrian powers, that the General
was tough. Next, it was observed that he was as
tough as hickory. Then he was called *Hickory*.
Lastly, the affectionate adjective ' old ' was prefixed, and the General thenceforth rejoiced in the
completed nickname, usually the first-won honour
of a great commander."

Of naval sobriquets we shall mention only three.
Commodore John Byron, the circumnavigator (born

1723, died 1786), was popularly known as **Foul Weather Jack** because, it was said, he never enjoyed a fine passage throughout the whole of his experience. Admiral Edward Vernon (born 1684, died 1757), to whom reference is made in our article on "SPIRITS," was called **Old Grog,** because he wore a "Grogram" coat in "dirty weather" [*see* GROGRAM]. Admiral Sir Henry Digby received his well-known sobriquet of **The Silver Captain** under the following interesting circumstances:—On the October 14, 1799, when commanding the frigate *Alcmene,* on a cruise off the Spanish coast, he shaped his course for Cape St. Vincent, and was running to the southward, in the latitude of Cape Finisterre. Twice during the night he rang his bell to summon the officer on the watch, and asked him if any person had been in the cabin. " No, sir ; nobody," was the answer. " Very odd," rejoined Sir Henry. " Every time I dropped asleep I heard somebody shouting in my ear, ' Digby! Digby! go to the northward; Digby! Digby! go to the northward!' I shall certainly do so. Take another reef in your topsails, haul your wind, tack every hour till daybreak, and then call me." These orders were strictly carried out, and the frigate was tacked at four, at five, at six, and at seven o'clock. She had just come round for the last time when the man at the masthead called out, "Large ship on the weather-bow, sir!" On nearing her a musket was discharged to bring her to. She was quickly boarded, when she proved to be a Spanish vessel laden with dollars, in addition to a large cargo of cochineal and spices. By this capture therefore, the fortunate dreamer secured, as his (Captain's) share of the prize-money, the sum of £40,730 18s.; the lieutenants each £5,091 7s. 3d.; the warrant officers each £2,468 10s. 9½d.; the midshipmen each £791 17s. 0¼d.; and the seamen and marines each £182 14s. 9½d. The captured treasure was said to have been so weighty that sixty-three artillery tumbrils had to be requisitioned for the purpose of transporting it from the vessel to Plymouth Citadel.

MONEY.

THE word **Money** owes its existence to *Moneta*, one of the surnames of Juno, in who se temple the first coinage of the Romans took place. **Mint** claims the same etymology, being a contraction of the Latin *moneta*, brought about through the Anglo-Saxon *mynet*. By **Sterling Money** is meant the standard coin of Great Britain, and for this reason :—During the reign of King John the merchants of the Hansa Towns, of which the inhabitants were commonly described as Esterlings, because they resided in the eastern portions of Germany, having long been noted for the purity of their coinage, the king invited a number of them over to this country for the purpose of reforming and perfecting our coinage. The invitation was accepted ; and ever afterwards good English money received the name of Esterling or sterling money.

A **Guinea** was an English gold piece first struck in 1663 out of gold brought from the coast of Guinea, West Africa. Its value has been subject to fluctuations at different periods. Thus, in 1663 it was worth 20s. ; in 1695, 30s. ; in 1717, 21s. ; in 1810, 22s. 6d. ; and in 1816, 26s. The coinage of guineas was discontinued July 1, 1817. **A Sovereign** is so called because when originally coined, during the reign of Henry VIII., it bore a representation of that sovereign in his royal robes. **A Crown-piece** when first introduced displayed a crown on its reverse side. The **Florin** took its name from Florence, in which city it was struck as long ago as the thirteenth century. Its reverse side has always borne a representation of a lily, emblematical of "The City of Flowers." The term **Shilling** traces its origin in the Anglo-Saxon *scilling*, the Icelandic *skillinge*, and the Gothic *skilliggs*, in each case denoting the twentieth part of a pound, as at present. A **Penny,** so called from the Anglo-Saxon *penig*, and Danish *pennig* (whence the modern German **Pfennig** has been derived), originally denoted a copper coin of full value ; a **Halfpenny,** the half of a penny ; and a **Farthing,** a corruption of the Old English *fourthling*, denotes a penny divided into four parts. We must not omit to mention that in olden times only penny-pieces were struck; and these were deeply indented in the form of a cross—exactly, in fact, after the manner of our Good Friday buns ; so that when half-pennies or farthings were required the pennies could be broken into two or four portions without difficulty.

Among coins other than those now current in this country we may mention the **Ducat,** or Duke's Money, specially struck for circulation in the Duchy of Apulia in the year 1140, and which bore this beautiful inscription : " Sit tibi Christi, datus, quem

tu regis, iste ducatus " (" May this duchy which
You rule be devoted to You, O Christ ") ; and the
Noble, so called on account of the superiority of its
gold.   During the reign of Henry III. this gold piece
found its way into England under the name of **Rose-
Noble,** owing to the impression of a rose on its
reverse side ; but in the reign of Henry VIII.,
simultaneous with the substitution of the figure of
St. George, it was designated a **George-Noble.**
The value of this coin at both periods was six-and-
eightpence.   The current value of an **Angel,** so
styled from the angel on its reverse side, was, when
introduced in the reign of Henry VI., six-and-eight-
pence ; but at the accession of Elizabeth it had
increased to ten shillings.

The **Thistle-crown** of James VI. of Scotland
(James I. of England), value four shillings, was so
called because it had a rose on one side and a thistle
on the other; both surmounted by a crown.   The
Scottish sovereign of this period was styled a
Jacobus, the Latinized form of the King's name.
After the union of the two countries it became, of
course, current in England also ; but in the two succeeding reigns it was denominated a **Carolus,** the
Latin for the name of Charles.   A French gold
coin long current in Scotland was the **Dolphin,**
which derived its name from the fact of its introduction by Charles V., who was also Dauphin of
Vienne.   The French **Louis d'or** (a louis of gold)
was first struck in the reign of Louis XIII. ;
this was superseded by the **Napoleon,** during the

consulate of Napoleon Bonaparte. The **Franc** originally denoted the silver coin of the Franks. The term **Dollar** is a British modification of the German Thaler, an abbreviation of Joachim's-Thaler; by which was implied a piece of money struck out of the silver discovered in the Thal, or Valley, of St. Joachim, France, about the year 1518. The silver drawn from this valley being of superior quality, it was coined into ounce pieces, which received the name of **Joachims-Thalers**; but all other ounce pieces subsequently struck from silver obtained elsewhere were simply called **Thalers.** The **Kreuzer,** now superseded, owed its name to the cross on its reverse side.

Wood's Halfpence was the designation of an inferior copper coinage circulated in Ireland by a certain William Wood, under a patent granted to him by George I. The withdrawal of the patent was eventually procured owing to the denunciations of Dean Swift in the mysterious "Drapier's Letters." The legal tender notes of the United States are commonly styled **Greenbacks,** from the colour of the device imprinted on the back of them. Bank of England notes formerly bore the name of **Abraham Newlands** from the signature of the chief cashier.

By the term **Bullion,** remotely derived from the Low Latin *bulla*, a seal, and, more directly, from the Old French *bullione*, the Mint, is meant the stock of the precious metals formed into bars and stored in the strong rooms of the Bank of England in readiness for coinage. Money vested in Government securities is

known as **Stock,** or **Government Stock,** in allusion
to the origin of the term, viz., the Anglo-Saxon
stocc, a trunk, a stick; because prior to the year 1782,
when the practice was abolished, the official acknowledgment of money received on behalf of the Government was written on both sides of a broad piece of
wood, which was then cut in two; and the one portion, called the Stock, was delivered to the person
lending the money, the Counterstock being retained
at the Tally Office. The instrument of reckoning
in this manner was styled the **Tally,** in accordance
with the French verb *tailler*, to cut; while the cor-
respondence of the Stock and Counterstock, or, in
other words, the two portions of the Tally, furnished
the origin of the modern phrase " to tally," as well
as the designation TALLYMAN, or a trader who lets
out goods, principally clothing, on the system of payment by weekly instalments. The word **Consols** is
a contraction of " Consolidated Annuities," or the
funded portion of the National Debt. The fund
which provides for the annual reduction of the latter
is styled the **Sinking Fund.** The French State
Loans known as **Tontines** perpetuate the name of
Lawrence Tonti, a Neapolitan *protégé* of Cardinal
Mazarine, who projected the scheme in 1653. The
annual statement by the Chancellor of the Exchequer
of the finances of this country is called the **Budget,**
agreeably to the French *bougetta*, a little bag; because
formerly the various documents were presented to
Parliament in a leathern bag.

SPIRITS.

RUM is a native West Indian term for a spirit distilled from cane-juice; **Whisky** is an English rendering of the Irish **Uisquebaugh,** derived from the two Gaelic words *uisge,* water, and *beatha,* life; **Brandy** is a corruption of the Old English *brandwine,* literally burnt wine; while **Gin** is short for Geneva, where this spirit was first distilled. **Hollands** is the popular English name for Dutch gin. **Cognac,** a French brandy of the best quality, owes its designation to the town of which it forms the staple industry; and **Nantes** to the port where it is shipped. **Old Tom** was named after Tom Chamberlain, the senior partner in Messrs. Hodges' well-known distillery.

The term **Punch** traces its origin to the Hindoo *pautsch,* signifying five, because this favourite concoction originally consisted of five ingredients, viz., arrack, sugar, tea, lemons, and water; whereas **Toddy** is a western corruption of *taudi,* the native Hindoo name for palm-juice. The word **Grog** perpetuates the memory of " Old Grog," the nickname of Admiral Edward Vernon, who first ordered his sailors to dilute their rum with water [*see* OLD GROG].

17

Scotch whisky is usually styled **Mountain Dew,**
from the fact that in former times it was often distilled in the mountains in order to escape the watch-
fulness of the excise officers. The superior Scotch
whisky known as **Glenlivet** derives its name from
the district in which it is distilled. The popular
LL Whisky originated under the following circumstances : When the Duke of Richmond was
Lord Lieutenant of Ireland, he one day, in the year
1807, sent to various Dublin distilleries for samples
of their best whisky ; and preferring that furnished
by Messrs. Kinahan, his Grace ordered a large vat
in which this particular quality of the spirit was
kept to be reserved for his own use. Accordingly, the
letters " LL," signifying Lord Lieutenant, were
painted on the vat ; and ever since Messrs. Kinahan's whisky of the same quality has borne the
name of " LL Whisky."

LONDON STREETS AND SQUARES.

FLEET STREET received its name from the Fleet, once a swift-flowing stream, now converted into a sewer. **Mitre Court, Falcon Court,** and **Red Lion Court** were designated after old taverns respectively bearing these signs. **Bolt Court** was so called from the " Bolt-in-Tun," an ancient coaching-house, transformed into a railway goods receiving office standing on the opposite side of the way. **Johnson's Court** did not receive its title from Dr. Johnson, who lived in it for some time, but from the owner of the property. **Wine Office Court** originally contained an office where wine licences were issued. **Shoe Lane** received this designation from the traditional account that when the Devil ran away with Lady Hatton [*see* HATTON GARDEN] he dropped one of her shoes in Shoe Lane and her cloak in **Cloak Lane,** near Cannon Street. **St. Bride Street** and **Bride Lane** owe their names to the Church of St. Bride close by. **Salisbury Court** occupies the site of an ancient palace of the Bishops of Salisbury. **Dorset Street** and **Dorset Buildings** carry us back in fancy to the **Dorset Gardens**

Theatre, erected in the grounds attached to the residence of the Earl of Dorset in the early days of the Restoration. **Whitefriars Street** marks the western boundary of the monastery of the Carmelites, or White Friars, built in 1245. The whole district of Whitefriars formerly comprised a Sanctuary infested by debtors and lawbreakers ; on which account it bore the name of **Alsatia,** in allusion to the French province of Alsace, long notorious for its intestine strife and political disaffection. **Bridge Street** is a modern thoroughfare leading to **Blackfriars Bridge** and **Blackfriars Road,** so called from the monastery of the Dominicans or Black Friars established on the site of **Printing House Square** and the *Times* office, about the year 1276. **Water Lane** was originally a narrow lane winding down to the Thames.

Ludgate Hill derived its name from the old Lud Gate, built by King Lud in the year 66 B.C. on the spot where the London, Chatham, and Dover Railway now crosses this busy thoroughfare. The gate was removed in 1760. **La Belle Sauvage Yard** was formerly the coachyard of the celebrated Inn of this name. **The Old Bailey** is a corruption of *Bail Hill,* which contained the residence and court of the Bail, or Bailiff, from very early times. The **Broadway** was doubtless considered a fine thoroughfare in the days when London streets generally were so narrow that opposite neighbours could shake hands out of their top-story windows. **Friar Street** was designated after the Black Friars'

Monastery. **Sermon Lane** is a corruption of " Shere-moniers' Lane," in which stood the office of the money-shearers or clippers at the time when the Mint was in this neighbourhood. **Paul's Chain** owed its name to a chain formerly drawn across its northern extremity the while service was held in St. Paul's. **Old Change** was originally known as " The King's Exchange" on account of the building where the bullion was stored convenient to the Money-shearers' Office and the Mint. **Paternoster Row** received its name from the stationers who sold religious texts, prayer-books, and rosary beads, formerly called *Paternosters* in this street. **Ave Maria Lane, Creed Lane,** and **Amen Corner,** being of later date, their designation to complete the religious metaphor was perhaps natural. **Warwick Lane** stands on the site of a magnificent palace owned by the Beauchamps, Earls of Warwick. **Ivy Lane** contained the ivy-clad houses of the prebendaries attached to St. Paul's Cathedral. In **Panyer Alley** may be seen a curious stone let into the wall of the middle house on the east side, upon which are chiselled the rude figure of a boy seated on a pannier or basket, and a distich reminding the pedestrian that this is the highest ground in the City. The alley was a standing-place for bakers with their panniers at the time when a corn market was held at the western extremity of Cheapside.

Cheapside properly denotes that side of the Cheap where the rich goldsmiths had their shops. The term *cheap* is Saxon for a market, derived from *ceapan*, to buy. The Old English spelling of the name of this locality was **Chepe. Ironmonger Lane** was the regular habitation of the artificers in iron in the reign of Edward I.; **Bread Street** of the bakers; and **Friday Street** of the fishmongers who supplied the fast-day markets. **Milk Street** was the ancient milk market. **Gutter Lane** is a corruption of "Guthurun Lane," so called after a wealthy Danish burgher. **Foster Lane** contains the Church of St. Vedast (otherwise St. Foster), Bishop of Arras in the French province of Artois, in the time of Clovis. **Wood Street** was anciently inhabited by turners and makers of wooden cups and dishes and measures. **Lawrence Lane** received its name from the Church of St. Lawrence in **Gresham Street,** which perpetuates the memory of Sir Thomas Gresham, merchant and founder of the Royal Exchange (born 1519, died 1579), because **Gresham College,** established by him in his own mansion, on the site of the present **Gresham House,** Old Broad Street, was removed here in 1843. **Lad Lane,** now absorbed in Gresham Street, was a corruption of "Our Lady Lane," so called from a statue of the Virgin. **Aldermanbury** was so called from the original Guildhall that stood on its east side. The approach to the present Guildhall received the name of **King Street** in honour of Henry IV., in whose reign the edifice was opened. In **Basinghall Street** stood the mansion of Solomon Basing, Lord Mayor in 1216. **Coleman Street** preserves the memory of the first builder upon the land. The **Old Jewry** was the privileged quarter of the Jews, whose first synagogue was erected here in 1262. **The Poultry** comprised the shops of the scorchers and stuffers, who afterwards settled down in the **Stocks Market** (so called from the old stocks for public offenders that stood there), displaced by the building of the Mansion House in 1739. **Bucklersbury** was originally the property of a wealthy grocer named Buckle who owned a manor-house here ; the Anglo-Saxon word *bury* being applicable either to a town or to an inhabited enclosure. **King William Street** was named soon after William IV. opened the present London Bridge, on August 1, 1831. **Queen Victoria Street** was cut through in the reign of her present Majesty.

Cannon Street is a corruption of **Candlewick Street,** colloquially styled " Can'lwick Street," from the candlemakers who congregated in it. **Budge Row** received its name from the sellers of budge, or lambskin-fur, which at one time was greatly used as an ornamentation to their attire by scholars and civic dignitaries. **London Stone** marked the centre of the City during its occupation by the Romans in the year 15 B.C. **Watling Street** is a mispronunciation of " Vitellina strata," meaning the street of Vitellius, who at the time it was constructed occupied the Imperial throne. This was the great highway of the Romans, running from Dover, through Canterbury and London, direct to Cardigan in Wales. **Walbrook,** formerly written " Wall-brook," reminds us of the

pleasant stream of clear water that once ran along
the west side of this street and emptied itself into
the Thames.   **Crooked Lane** was so called from its
winding character.   **Swan Alley,** in Upper Thames
Street, derived its title from an ancient mansion of
the Beauchamps whose crest was a swan.   **Boss
Alley** calls attention to the fact that the executors
of Sir Richard Whittington erected a *boss*, or conduit, hereabouts in the long, long ago.   **College
Hill** is all that remains to remind us of the College
of St. Spirit and St. Mary founded on its site by the
same generous Lord Mayor and benefactor of the
public.   **Fye Foot Lane** is properly " five-foot
lane," the actual width of this thoroughfare at one
end ; while **Duck's Foot Lane** is a corruption of
"Duke's Foot Lane," signifying the private path
leading from the manor-house of the Dukes of
Suffolk in what is now **Suffolk Lane** down to the
water-side.   **Queenhithe** was so called because the
tolls collected at this *hithe*, or wharf, were claimed
as pin-money by Eleanor, queen of Henry II.
Dowgate is a modern spelling of " Dwrgate " (*dwr*
being Celtic for water), where, in the absence of
bridges, the Romans had a ferry across the river
to the continuation of Watling Street towards
Dover.   The **Steelyard** was the place where the
King's beam, or *Steel yard*, for weighing merchandise
was set up.   Foreigners who landed goods here
were, between the thirteenth and fifteenth centuries, known as THE STEELYARD MERCHANTS.
   Gracechurch Street, formerly corrupted into

" Gracious Street," received its name from an old church standing in a grass market hereabouts. **Fenchurch Street** recalls the church in the fens, or marshy land, on the north bank of the Thames. **Eastcheap** was the eastern *cheap* or market, as distinguished from Chepe or Cheapside. **Mincing Lane** is a corruption of " Mynchen Lane," denoting the tenements held by the *minichery*, a Saxon name for a nunnery, of St. Helen's, Bishopsgate Street. **Mark Lane** was originally styled " Mart Lane," from a fair held here from the earliest times. **Blind Chapel Court,** situated at the north-east corner of Mark Lane, carries the imagination back to " Blanch Appleton," the documentary description of a white stone manor belonging to a knight named Appleton, in the reign of Richard II. In **Rood Lane** stood an ancient *rood*, or cross, representing the dying Saviour. **Seething Lane** is a corruption of Sidon Lane ; and **Billiter Street** of Belzetti Street, commemorating the names of the original owners of, and builders upon, the land. The **Minories** marks the site of the Priory of the MINORESSES, or NUNS OF ST. CLARE (the Order founded in Italy by St. Clare in 1212) ; corresponding to the **Minims,** or Lesser Friars, founded by St. Francis de Paula in 1453. **Crutched Friars** was the Priory of the Crutched, or Crossed, Friars of the Holy Trinity [*see* RELIGIOUS ORDERS]. **Aldgate** received its name from the *Ald Gate*, the oldest of the City gates, taken down in 1760. Aldgate Pump, which stood beside the gate, still remains. **George**

Yard was formerly the inn yard of " The George."
Duke's Place preserves the memory of Thomas
Howard, Duke of Norfolk, beheaded in 1572, who
had inherited the property of the Crutched Friars
by marriage.

Leadenhall Street derived its title from the
Leadenhall Market, a corruption of " Leather
Hall," the leather-sellers' market of olden times. **St.
Mary-Axe** owes its name to the Church of St. Mary-
Axe which stood in it [*see* the article " LONDON
CHURCHES AND BUILDINGS "]. **Throgmorton
Street** and **Nicholas Lane** were both named after
Sir Nicholas Throgmorton, a wealthy London
banker, and the head of an ancient Warwick-
shire family, said to have been poisoned by Robert
Dudley, Earl of Leicester, in 1571. **Thread-
needle Street** is a corruption of " Three-Needle-
Street," so called from the arms of the Needle
Makers' Company. **Bartholomew Lane** was de-
signated after the Church of St. Bartholomew, at
the back of the Royal Exchange. **Lothbury**
was originally " Lattenbury," inhabited by the
workers in *latten*, a fine kind of brass or bronze, which
formed an important industry in the Middle Ages.
Cornhill was the ancient corn market. **St.
Michael's Alley,** where the first English coffee-
house was opened, took its name from the neighbouring church. **Finch Lane** is properly " Finke
Lane," in honour of Sir Robert Finke, who built the
Church of St. Bennet Finke, pulled down to enlarge
Gresham's Royal Exchange. **Change Alley,** a

contraction of "Exchange Alley," was in the year 1720 the busy centre of the South Sea Bubble. **Birchin Lane** is a corruption of "Birchover Lane," named after the builder.

Lombard Street constituted the colony of the Jews of Lombardy sent over to England by Pope Gregory IX. for the purpose of advancing money to those who were unable to pay the taxes so rigorously demanded throughout the country in 1229. **Austin Friars** contained the Priory of the Austin, or Augustin Friars. **Bishopsgate Street** was designated after the strong gate built by the good Bishop Erkenwald, son of Offa, King of the Saxons; and repaired by Bishop William in the reign of William I. **Great St. Helen's** comprises the ground anciently held by the Nuns of the Order of St. Helen. **Devonshire Square,** in this neighbourhood, marks the situation of the mansion of William Cavendish, second Earl of Devonshire, who died under its roof in 1628. **Artillery Lane** stands upon the old practising ground of the Tower Gunners prior to the seventeenth century. **Houndsditch** was the old ditch beyond the city wall, anciently considered by the inhabitants to be the proper depository for dead dogs. **Bevis Marks** is a corruption of "Bury's Marks," where stood the mansion and grounds of the Abbots of Bury. **Petticoat Lane,** also known as **Rag Fair,** is the central old clothes mart of the Jewish inhabitants of the metropolis. **Wormwood Street** and **Camomile Street** were so called on account of the herbs found **growing** among the Roman stones. **London Wall** defines the ancient boundary of Roman London. **Barbican, a** continuation of the old Roman Wall, is an English form of the Saxon *burgh kennin*, or postern tower. Here it was that the Romans placed sentinels by night and day to give notice of conflagrations in the City or of dangers from outside quarters. In **Great Winchester Street** stood the original **Winchester House,** built by the first Marquis of Winchester. **Old Broad Street** was in Elizabeth's reign the most fashionable thoroughfare in London, containing the mansions of the wealthiest city merchants. **Moorgate Street** was so called from the gate that divided the City from the moor, comprising the borough of Finsbury. **Beech Lane** was designated after Nicholas de la Beech, Lieutenant of the Tower during the reign of Edward III. **Cripplegate** is the narrow thoroughfare anciently graced (or disgraced) by a stone gate which received its name from the beggars and cripples who congregated around it. This affection for the old gate on the part of the cripples may be explained by the circumstance that the neighbouring church was dedicated to St. Giles, the patron of cripples. **Whitecross Street** and **Red Cross Street** were respectively denominated from a white and a red cross of stone, which defined the boundaries of the land belonging to the Knights Templars and the Knights Hospitallers. **Playhouse Yard** reminds us that the old " Fortune Theatre " stood here. **Jewin Street** was for centuries the only burying-ground permitted to the Jews of London. **Aldersgate Street** took its name from the old City gate, distinguished for several alder-trees that grew beside it. In **Bridgewater Square** stood the mansion, destroyed by fire in 1687, of the Egertons, Earls of Bridgewater. **Bartholomew Close** marks the situation of the cloisters of St. Bartholomew's Priory, of which the church still remains. **Cloth Fair** comprised the ancient rendezvous of the Flemish and Italian merchants for the annual sale of cloths. This was the real Fair, to which " Bartholomew Fair " was merely an adjunct designed for the amusement of the populace who came from all accessible parts of the country. **Duke Street** and **Little Britain** were so called because in olden times the Dukes of Brittany resided here. **Newgate Street** received its name from the latest of the City gates, which also lent its title to the gloomy prison hard by. **Bath Street** contained one of the Turkish Bagnios, or Baths, introduced in London as early as the year 1679. **King Edward Street** serves to remind us that the neighbouring Grammar School known as Christ's Hospital was established by Edward VI. **Giltspur Street,** formerly styled **Knightrider Street,** was so called from the Knights, distinguished by their gilt spurs, who passed through it on their way to the tournaments in Smithfield. **Pie Corner,** where the great Fire of London ceased its ravages in 1666, derived its name from an eating-house that rejoiced in the sign of " The Magpie." **Farringdon Street** and **Farringdon Road** perpetuate the memory of William Farrindon, citizen and goldsmith, who purchased the Aldermanry of the Ward still known by his name for twenty marks in 1279, and became Sheriff two years later. **Saffron Hill** owes its designation to the rich crops of saffron that grew on its site at the time when it formed the eastern portion of the grounds attached to Ely House, the London residence of the Bishops of Ely, which stood on the spot now marked by **Ely Place,** and bounded on the west by **Hatton Garden;** so called because, when the property became demised to the Crown, it was presented by Queen Elizabeth to Sir Christopher Hatton, who literally danced himself into Her Majesty's favour. **Snow Hill** was formerly described as " Snore Hill," from the fact that the stage-coach passengers intended for " The Saracen's Head " were generally fast asleep when they arrived at their destination.

Holborn is a contraction of " The Hollow Bourne," indicative of a stream in a hollow. In Domesday Book the name appears as " Holebourne." **Holborn Bars** marks the City boundary on its western side. **Leather Lane** was the recognized colony of the leather-sellers. **Fetter Lane** is a perversion of " Fewtor's Lane "—in other words, a lane infested by vagabonds in the days when it led to some pleasure gardens. The term was derived from the Norman-French *faitour,* signifying an evil-doer. **Brooke Street** (in which Chatterton, the boy-poet, ended his life by poison), and **Greville Street** preserve the name of Fulke Greville, Lord Brooke, Councillor to James I., whose house stood in the latter thoroughfare. **Gray's Inn Road** forms the eastern boundary of Gray's Inn. **Verulam Buildings,** Gray's Inn, facing Gray's Inn Road, received this title in honour of Lord Bacon, who was created Baron Verulam and Viscount St. Albans. **Furnival Street,** on the east side of Holborn Bars, owes its name to Furnival's Inn, which it faces. Until quite recently this street was designated **Castle Street,** from the old " Castle Inn," whose site it covers. The name of **Dyers' Buildings** memorializes the one-time existence of some almshouse erected hereabouts by the Dyers' Company. **Cursitor Street** received its title from the Cursitors' Office founded in this vicinity by the father of the great Lord Bacon. The Cursitors were those who issued writs in the name of the Court of Chancery. The word *cursitor* is a corruption of chorister. Anciently all the officers of the Court of Chancery were divines; and the Lord High Chancellor himself was the Ecclesiastical Keeper of the King's Conscience. **Chancery Lane** is a corruption of " Chancellor's Lane," originally containing the court and official residence of the Lord High Chancellor. **Southampton Buildings** occupy the site of Southampton House, which witnessed the death of Thomas, the last Earl of Southampton, Lord Treasurer of Charles II. Those sorry tenements, **Chichester Rents** supply the place of the old town mansion of the Bishops of Chichester. **Lincoln's Inn Fields** are situated on the east side of the Inn, or mansion, of Henry de Lacey, Earl of Lincoln, in the fourteenth century [*see* INNS OF COURT]. **Sardinia Street** takes its name from the **Sardinian Chapel,** the oldest Roman Catholic chapel in London, dating back to the year 1648, and originally the residence of the Sardinian ambassador. **Great Turnstile** and **Little Turnstile** are pleasant-sounding names, eminently suggestive of the rural character of this neighbourhood in bygone days. The turnstiles were set up to prevent sheep and cattle from straying out of Lincoln's Inn Fields into the public highway. **Great Queen Street** was so called in compliment to Queen Elizabeth, in whose reign it was first formed into a footway for pedestrians plodding westwards from Lincoln's Inn towards the narrow path, anciently designated, as the modern street still is, **Long Acre.** The word *Acre*, derived from the Greek *agros*, Latin *ager*, and Anglo-Saxon *acer*, means a ploughed or sown field. **Drury Lane** derived its name from Drury House, the town residence of Sir William Drury, K.G., one of our most able commanders in quelling the wars with Ireland. The house was situated where the Olympic Theatre now stands. **Denzil Street** and **Holles Street** were so designated by Gilbert, Earl of Clare, whose house occupied the site of **Clare Market,** in memory of his uncle Denzil, Lord Holles, one of the five members of the House of Commons whose persons Charles I. made an ineffectual attempt to seize. **Hart Street** and **White Hart Street** both owe their titles to " The White

Hart" Inn, demolished in the time of George I.
Catherine Street, Strand, and **Portugal Street,**
Lincoln's Inn Fields, were designated in honour of
Catherine of Braganza, queen of Charles II. **Serle
Street** received its name from Henry Serle, a
bencher of Lincoln's Inn, who left considerable
property in the parish of St. Clement-Danes when
he died in 1690. **Wych Street** was known in early
times as *Aldwyche*, denoting the road leading directly
from the Strand and the church just mentioned to
the "Old town," now known as Broad Street, St.
Giles's parish. **Holywell Street** took its title from
the Holy Well discovered on the eastern side of St.
Clement-Danes.

The **Strand** literally means the strand of the
Thames. At one time Somerset House and a few
other princely mansions only occupied its southern
side. **Thanet Place,** a secluded *cul de sac* comprising ten houses, opposite the Law Courts, was
named after the Earl of Thanet, to whom, previous
to 1780, the property belonged. **Palsgrave Place**
was so called in compliment to the Palsgrave
Frederick, King of Bohemia, who married the
Princess Elizabeth, daughter of James I., in 1612.
Devereaux Court received its title from Essex
House, which also gave its name to **Essex Street,**
the residence of Robert Devereaux, Earl of Essex,
the Parliamentary General. **Milford Lane** was in
olden times characterized by a rustic mill; and the
lane itself led down to a ford across the river.
Arundel Street, Norfolk Street, Surrey Street,

18

and **Howard Street,** stand upon the site of the town house and grounds of the Howards, Dukes of Norfolk, and Earls of Arundel and Surrey. **Savoy Street** leads to the Chapel Royal, the only remaining portion of the ancient Savoy Palace [*see* SAVOY CHAPEL]. **Wellington Street,** constructed in 1829–30, was named to complete the compliment partially bestowed upon the Duke of Wellington by the designation of **Waterloo Bridge,** opened June 18, 1817, or two years after the famous victory. **Bow Street** was so called on account of its bent shape when it was first laid out to connect the Strand with Oxford Street in 1637. **Covent Garden** is a corruption of Convent Garden, or the garden belonging to St. Paul's Convent. **York Street** and **James Street** were both named in honour of the Duke of York, afterwards James II. **King Street,** constructed in his reign, was designated after Charles I., and **Henrietta Street** after his queen, Henrietta Maria. In **Tavistock Street, Russell Street, Bedford Street,** and **Southampton Street,** we trace some of the family titles of one of the ancestors of the present ground landlord, viz., Thomas Wriothesley, Earl of Southampton, Marquis of Tavistock, Duke of Bedford, whose daughter is known in history as the celebrated Rachel, the wife of Lord William Russell, the patriot, beheaded in 1683. Southampton House, in which Lady Russell was born, stood in the street named after it. **Bedfordbury** originally denoted the enclosed property of the Bedford family.

Maiden Lane was so styled on account of a statue of the Virgin that stood at the corner of this thoroughfare at the time when it skirted the south wall of the Convent Garden. **Chandos Street** received its name from James Bridges, Lord Chandos, the ancestor of the " Princely Duke of Chandos." **Exeter Street** marks the situation of Exeter House and its grounds, the property of a lineal descendant of the great Lord Burleigh, after whom **Burleigh Street** was designated. **Cecil Street** and **Salisbury Street,** on the opposite side of the Strand, remind us that here stood Salisbury House, the residence of Robert Cecil, first Earl of Salisbury, one of the sons of Lord Burleigh just alluded to.

Adelphi is the Greek word for brothers. This collective title was chosen for the pleasantly situated little district which comprises **Adelphi Terrace, Adam Street, John Street, Robert Street,** and **James Street,** the work of the brothers Adam, after whose Christian names three of the streets were designated. Similarly, **George Street, Villiers Street, Duke Street,** and **Buckingham Street** preserve the memory of George Villiers, second Duke of Buckingham, of whose mansion the old gate built by Inigo Jones may still be seen. **Charing Cross** is a perversion of " Chère Reine Cross," so named from the memorial cross erected upon the spot where the body of Eleanor, the *dear queen* of Edward I., was last set down while on its way to Westminster Abbey. The present cross is

merely a model of the original demolished by the
Puritans in 1647. **Craven Street** is the property
of Lord Craven. **Northumberland Street** and
Northumberland Avenue owe their names to
Northumberland House, the town mansion of the
Dukes of Northumberland, taken down in 1874.

Trafalgar Square received its title from the
Nelson Column, set up in 1843, two years before the
Square itself was completed. **St. Martin's Lane**
was named after the parish church of St. Martin's-
in-the-Fields. **King William Street** was built
upon in the reign of William IV. The name of
Seven Dials arose from a column set up at the
diverging point of seven streets, and displaying as
many clock faces. Its object was to mark the limits
of St. Giles's and St. Martin's parishes. **Cranbourne Street** marks the course of a long, narrow
bourne, or stream, that formerly ran from Tyburn
by way of Brook Street, Grosvenor Square, and
across Leicester Fields into Long Acre, and thence
emptied itself into the Thames at the bottom of
Milford Lane. The first portion of the name was in
allusion to the long, slender neck and legs of the
crane. **Leicester Square** (formerly demomin-
ated **Leicester Fields**) derived its name from
Leicester House, the noble mansion built on its
east side by Robert Sidney, Earl of Leicester, in
1636. On the site of **Coventry Street** stood the
mansion of Henry Coventry, Secretary of State in
the reign of Charles II. **Great Windmill Street**
reminds us of the old windmill that stood hereabouts

a couple of centuries ago. It was not until January, 1831, that the hay market, properly so called, was removed from the spacious thoroughfare still known as the **Haymarket**. **Jermyn Street** was named after Henry Jermyn, Earl of St. Albans, whose residence, St. Alban's House, stood on its north side. In **Arundel Street** we have one of the family titles of the ground landlord, Lord Arundel of Wardour. **Orange Street** was designated in honour of the Prince of Orange, afterwards William III. **Panton Street** perpetuates the memory of Colonel Thomas Panton, a notorious gamester, whose daughter married into the Arundel family. **Suffolk Street** marks the situation of the old town mansion of the Earl of Suffolk.

Spring Gardens, during the days of the Stuarts, contained an ingenious contrivance by which any person stepping upon a hidden spring was suddenly immersed in a shower of water. **Pall Mall** is a modern spelling of *paille maille*, the title of a French game at ball, somewhat similar to our croquet, first played in this thoroughfare — then open to St. James's Park — about the year 1621. **Carlton House Terrace** stands on the site of Carlton House, the palace of Frederick, Prince of Wales, the father of George III. **King Street, St. James's Street,** and **St. James's Square** were designated in honour of James I. **Bury Street** is properly "Berry Street," after the name of its builder.

The **Green Park** deserves its title on account of its verdure, so refreshing to the eye. **Hyde Park** anciently comprised the manor of Hyde held by the Abbots of St. Peter's, Westminster, but claimed by the Crown on the dissolution of the monasteries. **Hyde Park Corner** defines the position of the old toll-gate at the western extremity of London. **Rotten Row** is a corruption of *route du roi*, the French for "route of the King," to the historic royal residence at Kensington. **Albert Gate, Queen's Gate,** and **Prince's Gate** are of modern date, named in honour of the royal personages indicated. The **Marble Arch** is an imposing structure of white marble originally erected in front of Buckingham Palace in 1830, and removed to its present position in 1851. **Rutland Gate** was designated after the mansion of the Dukes of Rutland hard by. **Cumberland Gate** and **Duke Street,** Grosvenor Square, were both named after the Duke of Cumberland, brother to George III. **Grosvenor Gate, Grosvenor Street,** and **Grosvenor Square** preserve the memory of Sir Richard Grosvenor, Grand Cup-bearer to George II., who died in 1732. The ancestral line of the Gros-venors may be traced back to *Le Gros Veneur*, "the chief hunter," to the Dukes of Normandy prior to the Conquest. **Stanhope Gate, Great Stanhope Street,** and **Chesterfield Street** received their names from **Chesterfield House,** the residence of Philip Stanhope, Earl of Chesterfield, of epistolary fame. **Park Lane** was formerly a narrow lane skirting the east side of the Park. **Portugal Street** was named in honour of the queen of Charles II. **Chapel Street** owes its designation to its proximity to Grosvenor Chapel. **Hamilton Place** perpetuates the name of Colonel James Hamilton, Ranger of Hyde Park, and boon companion of Charles II.

That fine thoroughfare known as **Piccadilly** was designated after " Piccadilla Hall," its most westerly building during the reign of Elizabeth, and utilized as a depôt for the sale of the then fashionable PICCADILLY LACE, so called on account of its little spearlike points, *piccadilly* being the diminutive of *pica*, a pike, a spear. In the succeeding reign of James I., the high ruff worn by males was styled a piccadilly, though the lace had disappeared from its edge. **Curzon Street** was named after George Augustus Curzon, third Viscount Howe, the ground landlord. **Charles Street** and **Queen Street** were first built upon in the reign of Charles II., in honour of whom and his queen they were designated. **Shepherd Street, Shepherd's Market,** and **Market Street** faithfully preserve the memory of the owner of the land upon which the ancient " May Fair " was held. **Hay Hill, Hill Street,** and **Farm Street** mark the situation of an old farm that stood upon the lands of John, Lord Berkeley of Stratton, an able officer in the army of Charles I., whose titles are perpetuated in **John Street, Berkeley Square, Berkeley Street,** and **Stratton Street**; while **Bruton Street** refers to the family seat of the Berkeleys, situated at Bruton, Somersetshire. **Mount Street** marks the site of one of the western forts or bastions hastily formed by the Parlia-

mentarians in 1643 to resist an expected attack
upon the Metropolis from this side by the Royalists.
Clarges Street derived its name from the residence
of Sir Walter Clarges built in 1717, and afterwards
occupied by the Venetian Ambassador. In **Half-
Moon Street** stood an old tavern bearing the sign
of "The Half-Moon." **Arlington Street** and
Bennett Street were named after Henry Bennett,
Earl of Arlington, whose town house was situated
on the site of the former thoroughfare. **Dover
Street** was so called in memory of Henry Jermyn,
Lord Dover, who died in it in 1782. **Albemarle
Street** contained the residence of Christopher Monk,
second Duke of Albemarle, acquired from the Earls
of Clarendon. **Old Bond Street,** of which **New
Bond Street** is a modern continuation, received its
name from the Bond family, now extinct. The land
upon which it stands was the property of Sir Thomas
Bond, Comptroller of the Household of Henrietta
Maria, queen of Charles I. **Clifford Street** preserves the memory of Elizabeth Clifford, who
became the wife of Richard Boyle, Earl of Burlington (died 1753), after whom **Old Burlington Street,**
and subsequently, **New Burlington Street** were designated. In **Cork Street** resided Lord Cork, one
of the four brothers of the Boyle family advanced to
the peerage at the same time. **Savile Row** was
named after Dorothy Savile, who became Countess
of Burlington and Cork, and inherited the property.
Vigo Street commemorates the capture of Vigo, in
Spain, by the British on several occasions in the

course of the seventeenth and eighteenth centuries. The street dates back to the year 1720. **Sackville Street,** built in 1679, serves its purpose as perpetuating the memory of the witty Charles Sackville, Earl of Dorset, whose friends were unwilling that his fame should be allowed to die. **Air Street,** Piccadilly Circus, was at the time of its erection in the year 1659 one of the most westerly, and consequently, open streets of the town. **Swallow Street** is a corruption of " Slough Street," at one time a miry thoroughfare much infested by footpads. **Vine Street** recalls the ancient vineyard belonging to the Abbey at Westminster, situated here.

Regent Street was named by John Nash, the architect, after his royal patron, the Prince Regent. It was commenced in 1813. **Conduit Street** received its name from the conduit or spring-head set up in the meadow formerly known as " Conduit Mead," now swallowed up by Old Bond Street. **Maddox Street** was built by one Maddox in 1720. **Brook Street** reminds us of the pleasant stream that wound its way from Tyburn down to Leicester Fields, where it was designated the Cranbourne, and ultimately spent itself in the Thames. **Mill Street** affords us an additional memory of the rurality of London in bygone times. **George Street** (also **St. George's Church), Hanover Street,** and **Hanover Square** were designations in honour of the Hanoverian succession in the person of George I. **Davies Street,** connecting Berkeley Square with Oxford Street, received its name in compliment to Miss Mary Davies, the heiress of Ebury Manor, Belgravia, who carried that estate by her marriage into the possession of the Grosvenors.

Crossing Regent Street, **Argyll Street** marks the situation of the old town mansion of the Dukes of Argyll. **Marlborough Street, Great Marlborough Street,** and **Blenheim Street** were so called in honour of the Duke of Marlborough, the victor of Blenheim. **Wardour Street** is in allusion to the family seat of the ground landlord, Lord Arundel of Wardour. **Nassau Street** was named in compliment to the royal House of Nassau, from which the Prince of Orange claimed his descent. **Golden Square** is a corruption of Gelding Square, derived from an adjacent inn sign, " The Gelding." **Shaftesbury Avenue** is a modern thoroughfare named after Anthony Ashley Cooper, seventh Earl of Shaftesbury, who performed the opening ceremony but a short time before his death, which occurred in 1885. **Windmill Street** furnishes another pleasant reminder of green pastures and rural delights. **Old Compton Street** was built in the reign of Charles II. by Sir Francis Compton. **New Compton Street** and **Dean Street** derived their names from Bishop Compton, Dean of the Chapel Royal, Savoy, who originally possessed the living of St. Anne's, Soho. **Gerrard Street** and **Macclesfield Street** perpetuate the memory of Gerard, Earl of Macclesfield, the owner of the site at the time when buildings were first put up hereabouts in 1697. **Greek Street** was so called from the Greek mer-

chants who colonized this neighbourhood, and for
whose spiritual benefit a Greek church was erected
hard by. **Carlisle Street** was designated after the
Howards, Earls of Carlisle, a branch of the ducal
house of Norfolk, whose family mansion stood on
the east side of what is now Soho Square about the
middle of the last century.

Hanway Street, situated on the north side of
Oxford Street, received its name from Jonas Hanway,
who was the first to carry an umbrella through the
London streets. This occurred in the year 1750.
Rathbone Place, a somewhat exclusive thoroughfare, supporting its own police, was built by a Captain Rathbone in 1718. **Newman Street** and
Goodge Street retain the names of their speculative
builders. **Castle Street** took its title from an inn
sign at the corner of Oxford Market. **Wells Street**
is properly "Well Street," so called after Well in
Yorkshire, the seat of the Strangeways family, from
whom Lady Berners, the original ground landlady
of **Berners Street,** descended. In **Foley Street**
stood Foley House, the town mansion of Lord Foley.
Charlotte Street received its name in honour of
the queen of George III. **Bolsover Street, Great
Titchfield Street, Titchfield Street, Grafton
Street, Cleveland Street, Fitzroy Square,
Euston Square, Euston Road,** and **Southampton Street,** are all designated after family names of
the Fitzroys, Dukes of Grafton, Earls and Lords of
Southampton, the ground landlords. Euston is the
seat of the Earl of Euston, son of the Duke of

Grafton and Marquis of Titchfield, situated at
Thetford, in the county of Norfolk; while Bolsover
is the Derbyshire seat of the Graftons. **Tottenham
Court Road** anciently comprised the manor of
Totten, or Totham, held by William de Tottenhall
in the reign of Henry III. In Elizabeth's time the
manor was described as " Tottenham Court." The
lease fell into the possession of Charles Fitzroy,
second Duke of Grafton, by right of his mother,
Lady Isabella Bennett, who inherited it.

Oxford Street, formerly styled Oxford Road,
**Oxford Market, Mortimer Street, Harley Street,
Edward Street,** and **Wigmore Street,** derived
their names from Edward Harley, Earl of Oxford
and Mortimer, created Baron Harley of Wigmore
Castle in Herefordshire in 1717, the owner of the
estate. **Cavendish Square, Old Cavendish
Street, New Cavendish Street, Holles Street,**
and **Henrietta Street,** preserve the memory of
Henrietta Cavendish, wife of the second Lord
Harley, and only daughter and heiress of John
Holles, the last Duke of Newcastle, who by her
marriage carried all this property into the family of
the Harleys. Her daughter, Lady Margaret Cavendish, became in her turn the wife of William Bentinck, second Duke of Portland; in honour of which
connection there have been designated the various
thoroughfares known as **Bentinck Street, Margaret Street, Duke Street, Duchess Street,
Portland Place,** and **Great Portland Street.
Welbeck Street** was named after Welbeck Abbey,

in Northamptonshire, the seat of the Portland family; while **Clipstone Street** and **Carburton Street** were respectively designated after villages, the one in Nottinghamshire, the other in Northamptonshire, included in the ducal estate. **Wimpole Street** repeats the name of the seat of the Harleys situated on the borders of Herefordshire and Cambridgeshire, and purchased by Lord Chancellor Hardwicke in the last century. **Stratford Place** was built in 1775 by Edward Stratford, second Lord Aldborough, on ground leased from the Corporation of London for the purpose. The erection of **Queen Anne Street** dates from the reign indicated by its name. **Mansfield Street** is all that is left to remind us of the town residence of the Earl of Mansfield. **Langham Place** and **Langham Street** were named after Sir James Langham, whose mansion and grounds occupied the site of the latter. **Vere Street** recalls the existence of the De Veres, who for centuries held the Earldom of Oxford previous to the Harleys. **Duke Street, Manchester Street,** and **Manchester Square,** comprise the property of the Duke of Manchester. **Spanish Place** was originally so called from the residence of the Spanish Ambassador during the last century. **Chandos Street** derived its name from the mansion built by James Bridges, Duke of Chandos. **Hinde Street** perpetuates the memory of James Hinde, a speculative builder and one of the lessees of Marylebone Park more than a hundred years ago. **North Audley Street** and **South Audley Street**

point to the existence of Hugh Audley, a barrister
of the Middle Temple and owner of a landed estate
hereabouts worth a million of money; which, at his
death, in 1662, fell to Sir William Davies, Lord Mayor
of London, the father of Miss Mary Davies already
alluded to in connection with Davies Street and
Ebury Manor, Belgravia.

Old Quebec Street commemorates the capture
of Quebec by General Wolfe in 1759, about which
period this street was first built upon. **Seymour
Place** and **Upper Seymour Street** were designated
after the Seymours, from whom the Portmans are
descended. **Montague Street** and **Montague
Square** were so called in compliment to Mrs.
Montague of Blue Stocking fame, who, on becoming
a widow, took up her residence in Portman Square
close by. **Orchard Street** was designated in allusion to Orchard-Portman, one of the seats of the
Portmans, in Somersetshire. **Portman Square,
Portman Street, Berkeley Place, Upper
Berkeley Street, Lower Berkeley Street,
Bryanstone Square, Bryanstone Street, Wyndham Place, Wyndham Street, Blandford
Square, Blandford Street, Dorset Square,** and
Dorset Street, all have reference to the titles and
estate of the sole landlord of this neighbourhood,
viz., Edward Berkeley Portman, Viscount Portman
of Bryanstone, near Blandford, Dorsetshire, many
years M.P. for Dorset, and some time M.P. for
Marylebone. **Baker Street** received its name in
compliment to Sir Edward Baker of Ranston, a

valued neighbour of the Portmans in Dorsetshire. **Harewood Square** and **Harewood Street** mark the position of the town mansion of the Earls of Harewood. **Lisson Grove** stands on part of the land formerly known as *Lideston Green,* really a corruption of *Ossulton Green. Ossulton* is the name of a Hundred mentioned in Domesday Book, and preserved in **Ossulton Square,** close at hand, and also in **Ossulton Street,** Euston Road.

Regent's Park was named in honour of the Prince Regent, for whom it was originally intended to build a palace on the ground now utilized as the Botanic Gardens. **Albany Street** and **Osnaburgh Street** perpetuate the memory of Frederick, second son of George III., nominally styled Prince-Bishop of Osnaburgh in Hanover, and created Duke of York and Albany, and Earl of Ulster. **Cumberland Market,** whither the hay-market was removed from what still bears the description of the Haymarket in 1831, received its name in honour of Ernest Augustus, Duke of Cumberland, one of the sons of George III., who subsequently became King of Hanover. **Munster Square** was so called in compliment to the eldest son of William IV., created Earl of Munster. **Park Street** is the direct approach from High Street, Camden Town, to the Regent's Park. **Brecknock Road, Brecknock Crescent, Bayham Street, Pratt Street, Jeffreys Street, Henry Street, Charles Street, Frederick Street, Edward Street, William Street,** and **Robert Street,** repeat the titles, family and christian names occurring in the family of the Earl of Brecknock, Marquis of Camden, the owner of the estate, who died in 1840. **Great College Street, College Place,** and **College Street,** are situated within a stone's throw of the Royal Veterinary College. **Oakley Square** owes its title to Oakley House, near Bedford; and **Ampthill Square** to Ampthill Park, in Bedfordshire, the names of two seats of the Bedfords; while **Harrington Square** was denominated after the Earl of Harrington, one of whose daughters became the wife of the seventh Duke of Bedford. **Mornington Crescent** and **Mornington Place** were named in honour of the Earl of Mornington, Governor-General of India, the brother of the Duke of Wellington; and **Granby Street** after John Manners, the popular Marquis of Granby. **Eden Street** covers the site of the old "Adam and Eve" Tea Gardens. **Skinner Street,** Somers Town, was built, and is still owned by, the Skinners' Company.

Pancras Road received its name from the parish church of St. Pancras. **Battle Bridge Road** marks the spot where the Romans defeated the Iceni, under Queen Boadicea, in the year 61. **York Road** owes its designation to the fact that the Great Northern Railway was originally styled "The London and York Railway." **Caledonian Road,** which extends northwards to **Caledonian Market,** was so called after the Royal Caledonian Asylum, founded for Scottish orphans in 1831. **Liverpool Street** and **Sidmouth Street** recall the names of two popular Lords of the Ministry, at the accession of George IV. **Burton Crescent** memorializes its builder. **Judd Street** comprises the property bequeathed by Sir Andrew Judd, Lord Mayor in 1551, to the endowment of a school at Tunbridge, Kent, his native place. **Great Coram Street** affords us a pleasant reminder that the Foundling Hospital owes its existence to the benevolence of Captain Thomas Coram in the year 1739. **Lamb's Conduit Street** preserves the name of William Lamb, a clothworker to whose enterprise " a faire conduit and standard," constructed in 1577, was due. **Harpur Street** received its title in honour of Sir William Harpur, Lord Mayor in 1562, whose property hereabouts, together with that now known as **Bedford Row,** High Holborn, was devoted at his death to the foundation of a school and other charitable purposes at Bedford, his native place.

Southampton Row and **Southampton Street, Great Russell Street, Russell Square, Bedford Square, Tavistock Square,** and **Tavistock Place,** were named after Thomas Wriothlesley, Earl of Southampton, Marquis of Tavistock, and Duke of Bedford, father of Rachel, who became the wife of Lord William Russell, the patriot, already alluded to in connection with Southampton Street, Strand. **Gordon Square** perpetuates the memory of Lady Georgina Gordon, daughter of Alexander, fourth Duke of Gordon, and wife of John, sixth Duke of Bedford, who had had for his first wife a daughter of the noble house of Torrington, memorialized by **Torrington Square. Montague Street** and **Mon-**

tague **Place** occupy two sides of the site of Old
Montague House, the nucleus of the British
Museum. **Brunswick Square** and **Mecklen-
burgh Square** were built and designated at the
time when it was considered the correct thing to
honour the Hanoverian succession in every possible
way: **Thurlow Place** was named in compliment
to Lord Chancellor Thurlow, whose house was
situated in **Great Ormond Street,** so called after
the British general and duke of that title. **Powis
Place** covers the ground formerly occupied by Powis
House, the town mansion of William Herbert,
Marquis of Powis, whose father was outlawed by
James I. **Bloomsbury Square** is properly "Lomesbury Square," marking the site of the manor-house
described in olden times as " Lomesbury Village."
Hart Street received its name from " The White
Hart " Inn ; and **Red Lion Square** and **Red Lion
Street,** from " The Red Lion," both hostelries of
some importance in the coaching days. **Queen's
Square** was designated in honour of Queen Anne, in
whose reign it was laid out. **Kingsgate Street**
was so styled because the King used it on his way
to Newmarket ; while **Theobalds Road** led to
Theobalds, in Herefordshire, the favourite hunting
seat of James I.

Coldbath Square, Clerkenwell, marks the situation of the celebrated Cold Bath, fed by a spring discovered by Mr. Baynes in 1697. The surrounding
district before it was built over formerly bore the
name of **Coldbath Fields.** **Vinegar Yard** is a

corruption of the vineyard anciently belonging to the Priory of the Knights of St. John. **Ray Street** preserves the memory of Miss Ray, the mistress of Lord Sandwich, shot by her lover Hackman. **Rosoman Street** was designated after the enterprising Mr. Rosoman, who converted Sadler's Musick House into a theatre in 1765. **Aylesbury Street** in olden times skirted the wall of the garden attached to the town mansion of the Earls of Aylesbury. **Berkeley Street** derived its name from Berkeley House, the residence of Sir Maurice Berkeley, standard-bearer to Henry VIII., Edward VI., and Elizabeth. **Albemarle Street** was built during the period that witnessed the popularity of General Monk, Duke of Albemarle. In bygone times the whole of Clerkenwell received the opprobrious title of **Hockley-in-the-Hole**, the name of a place in Bedfordshire noted far and wide for its impassable and sloughy character. **Hockley** is an Anglo-Saxon term, denoting a muddy field. **Myddleton Square** and **Myddleton Street** perpetuate the memory of Sir Hugh Myddleton, the founder of the New River Waterworks, opened September 16, 1613. **Pentonville Road** owes its title to the *ville*, or rural mansion, occupied by Henry Penton, Esq., Lord of the Admiralty and M.P. for Winchester, on the spot where **Penton Street** now stands. Mr. Penton died in 1812. **St. John Street Road** took its name from the Priory of the Knights of St. John of Jerusalem, of which **St. John's Gate** is an interesting relic. **Windmill Street** marks the site of three large windmills erected in Finsbury Fields, on the mound formed by a thousand cartloads of human bones deposited there from the Charnel House, St. Paul's, by order of the Lord Protector Somerset, in 1549. **City Road** was the regular highway from the City to the " Angel " at Islington, and thence to the north of England, *viâ* Highbury and Highgate. **Shepherdess Walk** was originally a pleasant path leading through the open fields direct from Finsbury to St. Mary's parish church, Islington. **Golden Lane,** St. Luke's, received its name from the number of goldsmiths who formerly made this neighbourhood their residence. In **Curtain Road,** Shoreditch, stood the Curtain Theatre, opened in 1571, so called because it was the first playhouse to make use of a drop-curtain. Ben Jonson's " Every Man in his Humour " was produced here in 1596. By **Norton Folgate** is meant " the northern Falgate," the latter word being the old English description of a four-barred gate. THE FALGATE is a common inn sign in the rural districts. **Holywell Lane,** near Shoreditch Church, was so called on account of a miraculous well discovered here in ancient times. In **Nichols Square,** Haggerstone, lived John Nichols, the antiquary ; and in **Sutton Place,** Hackney, Thomas Sutton, the founder of the Charterhouse. **Queen Elizabeth's Walk,** Stoke Newington, marks the position of a house and grounds occupied by the Earl of Leicester, and often visited by Her Majesty. **Fleetwood Road** covers the site of Fleetwood House, the residence of Charles

Fleetwood, the Parliamentary general, and Deputy-Governor of Ireland.

Seven Sisters' Road, Holloway, received its name from seven trees, said to have been planted by seven sisters, near Tottenham, six of which grew erect; but the seventh presented a deformed appearance, because the sister who had planted it was a cripple. **Archway Road,** Highgate, is spanned by the wonderful high arch completed in 1813. **Flask Walk,** Hampstead, derived its name from " The Flask," a picturesque old inn close by. **Judges' Walk,** known also as **King's Bench Avenue,** was originally so called from a colony of judges and gownsmen of the City, who sought refuge here in tents during the Great Plague in 1665. **Fleet Road,** Haverstock Hill, affords us a pleasing remembrance of that little river, the Fleet, meandering through the fields in this neighbourhood, and eventually behind the older houses, on its way towards Battle Bridge, the City, and the Thames. **Dale Road** preserves the memory of Canon Dale, poet, and vicar of St. Pancras. **Barrow Road** and **Barrow Hill Place** commemorate the site of a battle between the Britons and Romans, and the sepulchre of the slain. The spot was formerly defined by a farmhouse that stood upon the actual barrow known as "Barrow Hill." **Abbey Road,** St. John's Wood, points to the existence of the ancient Abbey of the Holy Virgins of St. John the Baptist (*see* St. John's Wood). **Desborough Place,** Harrow Road, received its name from Desborough

House, the site of which it adjoins, and where lived
John Dessborough (or Desbrowe), the brother-in-law
of Oliver Cromwell.   **Church Street,** Paddington,
was so called from the parish church of St. Mary,
situated on the open space still known as **Paddington Green.   Nottingham Place** was designated
after the county in which the chief landed estates of
the Duke of Portland are situated; and **Weymouth
Street,** in compliment to Lord Weymouth, son-in-
law of the same nobleman.   **Paddington Street**
was formerly a narrow lane leading northwards into
Paddington Fields.

Craven Hill Gardens and **Craven Road,** Bayswater, occupy the site of the mansion and grounds
of the Lords Craven previous to the year 1700, when
they migrated to Craven House, Drury Lane.
Southwick Crescent and **Southwick Place**
received their names from Southwick Park, the seat
of the Thistlewayte family, formerly the joint lessees
of Paddington Manor.   **Orme Square** perpetuates
the memory of Mr. Orme, a print-seller, of Bond
Street, who bought the ground and commenced the
building of the Square in question.   **Ladbroke
Grove** and **Ladbroke Square** likewise bear the
name of the Ladbroke family, who built upon the
land leased to them for the purpose.   **Norland
Square,** Notting Hill, covers the site of Norland
House, a small, wooded estate, owned by one of the
Drummonds, the bankers, of Charing Cross, in the
reign of William IV.   **Kensington Gore** took its
name from Gore House, the residence of the

Countess of Blessington, long the central literary and social attraction in the Metropolis. In **Ennismore Place,** the second title of the Earl of Listowel, the ground landlord, is repeated. On part of the site of **Cromwell Road** stood the house and grounds owned by Richard Cromwell, the son of Oliver Cromwell. **Gloucester Road** derived its title from Oxford Lodge, the residence of the late Duchess of Gloucester, in the immediate vicinity. **Campden Hill** defines the estate belonging to Campden House, still standing in **Campden Square,** and originally occupied by Sir Baptist Hicks, who built **Hicks' Hall,** Clerkenwell, in 1612, afterwards created Viscount Campden. **Warwick Road, Warwick Gardens, Holland Road,** and **Earl's Court Road** are spacious modern thoroughfares, designated after the Earls of Warwick, the original owners of the estate known as **Earl's Court,** now in the possession of the Holland family. **Addison Road** reminds us that Joseph Addison, the poet, essayist, and dramatist, married the Dowager Countess of Warwick, and died in Holland House.

Cromwell Place, Putney, stands upon the site of Mr. Champion's house, the lodging of General Ireton, Oliver Cromwell's son-in-law, in 1646. **King's Road,** Chelsea, was named in honour of Charles II., who caused it to be made passable, chiefly for the benefit of the frequenters of "The World's End," then a popular house of entertainment. **Cheyne Row** and **Cheyne Walk** perpetuate the memory of Lord Cheyne, who held the

Manor of Chelsea in the seventeenth century. **Justice Walk** formerly contained the residence of a magistrate. **Marlborough Square** and **Marlborough Road** derived their names from a neighbouring tavern displaying the sign of "The Duke of Marlborough"; and **Keppel Street,** from "The Admiral Keppel," situated at the corner of Fulham Road. **Cadogan Street** and **Cadogan Square** remind us that the manor of Chelsea came into the possession of the first Earl of Cadogan by right of his marriage with the heiress of Sir Hans Sloane, after whom **Sloane Square, Sloane Street,** and **Hans Place** were named. **Danvers Street** was so called after Sir John Danvers, who introduced the Italian style of horticulture into England during the reign of Elizabeth. The street covers the site of Danvers House in which he lived.

Grosvenor Place and **Grosvenor Street** received their names from Sir Thomas Grosvenor, the ancestor of the Duke of Westminster, the ground landlord of the district collectively known as Belgravia; **Eccleston Street** and **Eccleston Square** from Eccleston, in Cheshire, the county in which the landed property of the Grosvenors chiefly lies; and **Belgrave Square** and **Belgrave Street** from the Viscountcy of Belgravia, the second title of the Duke of Westminster before he was raised to his superior titles. **Ebury Street** and **Ebury Square** mark the site of Ebury or Eabury Farm, an ancient manor inherited by Miss Mary Davies, already referred to when speaking of Davies Street, Oxford

Street, and carried into the family of the Grosvenors by her marriage. **Chester Square** reproduces the name of the city near which Eaton Hall, which gives its title to **Eaton Square,** the principal seat of the Duke of Westminster, is situated. **Lupus Street** perpetuates a favourite christian name in the Grosvenor family, retained in honour of Henry Lupus, created Earl of Chester soon after the Conquest. **St. George's Square** was designated after the adjacent church dedicated to St. George. **Lowndes Street, Lowndes Square,** and **Chesham Street,** Pimlico, are indebted for their title to Lowndes of the Bury, near Chesham, Buckinghamshire, the ground landlord, a descendant of William Lowndes, secretary to the Treasury during the reign of Queen Anne.

Vauxhall Bridge Road forms a connecting link between Vauxhall Bridge and **Victoria Street,** a gloomy modern thoroughfare named in honour of our present sovereign. **Birdcage Walk** comprised the place where the aviary of Charles II. was permanently located, under the superintendence of Master Edward Storey, the royal keeper, whose house covered the spot now styled **Storey's Gate** in his memory. **Queen Anne's Gate** derived its name from **Queen Anne's Square,** in whose reign this characteristic enclosure was built. **York Street** was designated in honour of Frederick, Duke of York, son of George III., who lived in it for a short time. **Delahay Street** compliments a family of this name long resident in St. Margaret's parish.

Rochester Row was denominated after the
Bishopric of Rochester, anciently combined with
the Deanery of Westminster, but separated in the
reign of George III. **New Bridge Street** leads to
the handsome bridge over the Thames, opened May
24, 1862. **Cannon Row** is properly " Canon Row,"
formerly the residence of the Canons of St. Stephen's
Chapel. **King Street** received its title because it
was the direct road between the Court and the
Abbey. **Princes Street,** a modern thoroughfare,
occupying the site of Old Westminster Mews, was
so called on account of its proximity to King Street.
Parker Street perpetuates the memory of Archbishop Parker, one of the principal benefactors of
Corpus Christi College, Cambridge. This street
was formerly known as Bennet Street, the old name
of the College. **Great George Street** covers the
ground originally occupied by the stable-yard of
" The George and the Dragon," a well-known
coaching house in bygone days. The name of **Broad
Sanctuary,** Westminster, reminds us of the protection which in olden times was afforded to criminals
of all degrees so long as they remained beneath the
shadow of a monastery or cathedral. **Abingdon
Street** contained the mansion of the Earls of Abingdon. **Holywell Street** owes its title to the name of
an estate of the Grosvenors in Flintshire, whose town
residence was displaced by the formation of this
street. **Barton Street** and **Cowley Street** were
both built by Barton Booth, the actor ; to the former
he gave his christian name, to the latter the name

of his favourite poet. **Marsham Street, Earl Street,** and **Romney Street** comprise the property of Charles Marsham, Earl of Romney; while **Old Pye Street** and **New Pye Street** commemorate the existence of Sir Robert Pye, who lived in the more modern portion of this neighbourhood known as **The New Way. Great Peter Street** recalls the fact that the Abbey of Westminster was dedicated to St. Peter. **Vine Street** marks the situation of the vineyard, and **Orchard Street** the orchard, anciently possessed by the Abbots. **Tothill Street** received its name from **Tothill Fields,** comprising the old manor of Tothill, a corruption of Toothill, or beacon hill; *toot* being derived from the Welsh *twt*, a rising. **Horseferry Road** needs no comment. **Millbank** derived its name from an old mansion belonging to the Grosvenor family, that stood on the site of an old mill which alone graced this portion of the Thames bank.

On the site of **Carlisle Lane,** Lambeth, stood Carlisle House, the residence of the Bishops of Rochester from the thirteenth century downwards. **Marlborough Road,** Peckham, covers the ground plot of a Marlborough House, the residence of John Churchill, Duke of Marlborough. **Hanover Street** was named in compliment to the accession of George I. **Basing Yard,** at the rear of Hanover Street, occupies the site of Basing House, well known during the Restoration. **Rye Lane** leads to the Rye, or Common. **Friern Place** and **Friern Road** define the locality of Friern Manor; while **Lordship**

Lane owes its designation to the lordship of the manor. **Effra Road,** Camberwell, marks the course of the little river Effra, now hidden, like the Fleet, from public view. **Newington Butts** denotes the archery grounds, formerly situated in the new town in the meadow. **Holland Street,** Southwark, preserves the name, at least in part, of an old manor, described as " Holland's Leaguer." **Great Suffolk Street** recalls the existence of Suffolk House, the residence of George Brandon, Duke of Suffolk ; **Winchester Yard,** of Winchester House, the habitation of the Bishops of Winchester ; and **Sumner Street,** of Dr. Sumner, Bishop of Winchester, one of the last occupants of the house just referred to. **Mill Lane** reminds us of an old windmill that stood here in less prosaic times ; and **Mint Street,** of the Mint established by Henry VIII. in Suffolk House, when that property became demised to the Crown. **Stony Street** and **Stones End** received their names from the stony nature of the ground ; the former having been the Roman continuation of Watling Street, south of the Thames, in a direct line to Dover. **Bear Garden,** situated at the corner of Sumner Street, marks the exact position of the old **Paris Garden,** a bear-baiting establishment, opened by Robert de Paris in the time of Richard I. **Bankside,** or the south strand of the Thames, is historically interesting on account of its theatrical associations.

Old Kent Road, which branches off at " The Bricklayers' Arms" into **Great Dover Street** and **Kent Street,** forms the great Kentish highway into

London. **Thomas Street** perpetuates the christian
name of the philanthropic founder of Guy's Hospital
hard by. **Grange Road** and **Grange Walk** occupy
the site of an old mansion known as " The Grange."
Spa Road derived its name from a spa, or mineral
well, discovered here in the long, long ago. **Russell
Street** preserves the memory of Richard Russell,
who, dying here in 1784, left the whole of his
estate to neighbouring charities. In **Tooley Street**
lived the three tailors who, according to tradition,
presented a petition to the House of Commons that
began with the words, " We, the people of England,
&c." During the Commonwealth this street
figured in documents as St. Tulie Street, but it is
properly designated St. Olaff Street, after the neighbouring church dedicated to St. Olaff or Olave, the
Scandinavian hero-prince. **Blue Anchor Road**
and **Blue Anchor Lane** received their names from
"The Blue Anchor," an old tavern that stood in the
latter thoroughfare ; while **Jamaica Road** recalls
a similar establishment, formerly situated on the
site of **Cherry Gardens**, a popular place of resort
in bygone times, known as " The Jamaica," after
the West Indian Island whence rum was shipped
and disembarked on the exact spot where the penny
steamboats now land and take up their passengers at
Cherry Gardens Pier. Lastly, **Evelyn Street,**
Deptford, was designated in honour of the present
head of the Evelyn family, descendants of John
Evelyn, the diarist, viz., William J. Evelyn, of
Wotton, who built the adjacent Church of St. Luke,
in the year 1872.

INDEX.

Index.